HEALTHY BREAKS

Wellness Activities for the Classroom

JENINE M. DE MARZO, EdD
Adelphi University

Human Kinetics

Library of Congress Cataloging-in-Publication Data

De Marzo, Jenine M., 1964-
  Healthy breaks : wellness activities for the classroom / Jenine M. De Marzo.
    p. cm.
  ISBN-13: 978-0-7360-8289-1 (soft cover)
  ISBN-10: 0-7360-8289-1 (soft cover)
  1. Health education (Elementary) 2. Social learning. 3. Education, Elementary-
-Activity programs. 4. Rest periods. I. Title.
  LB1587.A3D46 2010
  372.37'044--dc22

                              2009026850

ISBN-10: 0-7360-8289-1 (print)   ISBN-10: 0-7360-8744-3 (Adobe PDF)
ISBN-13: 978-0-7360-8289-1 (print)   ISBN-13: 978-0-7360-8744-5 (Adobe PDF)

Acquisitions Editor: Sarajane Quinn; **Developmental Editor:** Melissa Feld **Assistant Editors:** Rachel Brito, Elizabeth Evans; **Copyeditor:** Anne Rogers; **Permission Manager:** Dalene Reeder; **Graphic Designer:** Bob Reuther; **Graphic Artist:** Dawn Sills; **Cover Designer:** Keith Blomberg; **Cover photograph:** Courtesy of Jenine M. De Marzo; **Visual Production Assistant:** Joyce Brumfield; **Photo Production Manager:** Jason Allen; **Art Manager:** Kelly Hendren; **Associate Art Manager:** Alan L. Wilborn; **Illustrator:** Tammy Page; **Printer:** Versa Press

Printed in the United States of America   10   9   8   7   6   5   4   3   2   1

The paper in this book is certified under a sustainable forestry program.

Human Kinetics
Web site: www.HumanKinetics.com

United States: Human Kinetics
P.O. Box 5076
Champaign, IL 61825-5076
800-747-4457
e-mail: humank@hkusa.com

Canada: Human Kinetics
475 Devonshire Road Unit 100
Windsor, ON N8Y 2L5
800-465-7301 (in Canada only)
e-mail: info@hkcanada.com

Europe: Human Kinetics
107 Bradford Road
Stanningley
Leeds LS28 6AT, United Kingdom
+44 (0) 113 255 5665
e-mail: hk@hkeurope.com

Australia: Human Kinetics
57A Price Avenue
Lower Mitcham, South Australia 5062
08 8372 0999
e-mail: info@hkaustralia.com

New Zealand: Human Kinetics
Division of Sports Distributors NZ Ltd.
P.O. Box 300 226 Albany
North Shore City
Auckland
0064 9 448 1207
e-mail: info@humankinetics.co.nz

I have not always taken the most direct route or the most popular, yet I have managed to get somewhere. Thanks to my mom and dad for showing me the way; my husband, Chris, for walking beside me; and to Ari, Vic, and Gio who inspire me to continue moving forward.

CONTENTS

ACTIVITY FINDER

To help you find activities that are suitable for your students, the following table indexes the activities by several categories. They are categorized by National Health Education Standards, National Association for Sport and Physical Education Standards, grade level, activity type (quieting or meditative, esteem builder, sharing and social and emotional wellness, cooperative, inclusion, and energizers), and suggested time requirements. It is a quick and easy way to select a new activity or locate one that you have used before. The activities are listed alphabetically.

KEY

Suggested Time Requirements	Activity Type
5 to 10 minutes	Quieting or meditative
11 to 20 minutes	Esteem builder
	Sharing and social and emotional wellness
	Cooperative
	Inclusion
	Energizers

ACTIVITY	NHES STANDARDS	NASPE STANDARDS	GRADE LEVELS	ACTIVITY TYPE	SUGGESTED TIME REQUIREMENTS	PAGE #
ABCs and Me (Attitudes, Behaviors, Consequences)	1, 2, 5, 6	1, 2, 5, 6	2-6			22
All Me: Body Awareness	1, 2	1, 2, 3	K-3			2
All Together Now	4, 5, 6	1, 2, 3, 5, 6	4-6			54
Alphabet Relay	1, 4, 5, 6, 7, 8	1, 2, 3, 5, 6	1-6			56
Balloon Bounce	1, 4, 5, 6, 7	1, 2, 5, 6	K-3			36
Beach Ball Conversation	1, 2, 4, 7	1, 2, 5, 6	K-6			74
Beat the Clock	1, 4, 5, 6	1, 2, 3, 5, 6	3-6			45
Breathing, Visualization, and Emotional Expression	1, 2, 4, 7, 8	5, 6	2-6			18
Build a Better Letter	1, 2, 4, 5, 6, 7	1, 2, 3, 5, 6	K-6			58
Builders and Bulldozers	2, 4	1, 2, 3, 4, 5, 6	K-6			96
Crunch Time	1, 2, 4, 6	1, 2, 3, 4, 5, 6	K-6			52
The Curious Snail	1, 3, 5, 6, 7	1, 2, 5, 6	3-6			40
Deep Breathing	1, 4, 7	6	K-6			6
A Different View	1, 2, 4, 7	5, 6	2-6			26
Explain It to Me (Part 1)	2, 4, 8	5	3-6			66
Explain It to Me (Part 2)	2, 4, 5, 6, 7	1, 2, 3, 4, 5, 6	5-6			71
Extreme Hot Potato	4	1, 2, 3, 4, 5, 6	K-6			100
Friday Freak-Out	1, 7	1, 3, 4, 5, 6	K-6			92

(continued)

ACTIVITY	NHES STANDARDS	NASPE STANDARDS	GRADE LEVELS	ACTIVITY TYPE	SUGGESTED TIME REQUIREMENTS	PAGE #
The Hungry Snake	4, 5, 6	2, 5	K-3			43
I Feel Good, You Feel Good	1, 2, 4	5, 6	1-6			24
I'm in Control	1, 2, 4	6	4-6			4
Inside Out	1, 4, 5, 6	1, 2, 3, 4, 5, 6	K-6			47
Kopy Kat	2, 4	1, 2, 3, 5, 6	K-3			89
Map Quest	2, 4, 5, 6	1, 2, 5, 6	4-6			77
Meditative Breathing	1, 4, 7	5, 6	K-6			8
Monkey Business	1, 2, 3, 4, 5, 7	1, 2, 3, 4, 5, 6	K-3			94
(Not) Seeing Is Believing!	8	2, 5, 6	2-6			83
Nuts, Bolts, and Beads	8	2, 5, 6	2-6			81
Parachute Popcorn Blast	1, 4, 5, 6	1, 2, 3, 4, 5, 6	3-6			62
Progressive Muscle Relaxation	1, 2, 7	1, 2, 5, 6	K-6			11
The Qualities of Me! (Part 1)	1, 2, 3	5	3-4			31
The Qualities of Me! (Part 2): Good Friend Wanted	1, 2, 3	5	3-4			33
Spare Square Team Tag	4	1, 2, 3, 4, 5, 6	K-6			60
Stop, Drop, and Roll	1, 5, 7	1, 2, 3, 4, 5, 6	K-3			102
Stuck Like Glue Obstacle Course	1, 4, 5, 6, 7	1, 2, 5, 6	4-6			38
Under and Over Relays	1, 4, 5, 6	1, 2, 3, 4, 5, 6	K-6			98

ACTIVITY	NHES STANDARDS	NASPE STANDARDS	GRADE LEVELS	ACTIVITY TYPE	SUGGESTED TIME REQUIREMENTS	PAGE #
Untangle	1, 4, 5, 6	1, 2, 3, 5, 6	K-6			50
Visualization Activity: An Adventure Within	1, 6, 7, 8	5, 6	2-6			13
What Would You Do If . . .	1, 4, 5, 7	1, 2, 3, 4, 5, 6	K-3			87
Who Am I?	1, 4	5, 6	3-6			29
You Said What?	8	2, 5, 6	K-6			85

PREFACE

On any given day, at least one of my children would greet me after school with a chocolate mustache or the remnants of some other sweet treat they received in school as part of a birthday or seasonal celebration. At the same time, I saw my children's recess time being reduced dramatically. All of this occurred at about the same time that several federal agencies had begun to report their concerns regarding the prevalence of obesity in all segments of Western society and particularly among children and adolescents.

The idea for *Healthy Breaks* came as a result of a pursuit of two personal goals. The first was to address the food-centered celebrations that take place in my own children's school; the second was to advocate for increased health, wellness, and movement education for all children on a daily basis.

The material in this book provides classroom teachers, administrators, after-school programmers, counselors, coaches, and troop leaders with 5- to 10-minute healthy breaks that encourage all participants to become more mindful of their health, wellness, and activity levels throughout the day. Perhaps both the professionals and the children they serve will see past the traditions and use these activities as a treat or reward. These activities include original games that are suited for the kindergarten to 6th-grade crowd.

In the United States, the Child Nutrition and Women, Infants and Children (WIC) Reauthorization Act of 2004 (sec. 204 of P.L. 108-265), also known as the Federal Wellness Policy, was enacted in June 2006. This policy asserts that educational institutions must identify and implement better-defined nutrition education goals and increase physical activity for every school-age child. As a result, all local education agencies participating in the National School Lunch Program are required by law to embrace and operationalize these new recommendations as of June 2006. Educators, parents, after-school programmers, camp counselors, and coaches also were challenged to renew and expand their roles in providing and promoting health and wellness for all U.S. children. Other countries have started their own initiatives in the same direction. The Public Health Agency of Canada has recognized that the rapid increase in obesity, combined with low levels of physical activity, is a serious threat to the health of Canada's youth. In response, the Public Health Agency of Canada and the Canadian Society for Exercise Physiology developed physical activity guides that were launched in April 2002. In addition, sport and physical activity are now part of the tax system, the Children's Fitness Tax Credit, which began on January 1, 2007. The government of Canada proposed to allow a nonrefundable tax credit on eligible programs for up to $500 paid by parents to register a child in an eligible physical activity program. Eligible types of physical activity must contribute to cardiorespiratory endurance plus one or more of the following: muscular strength, muscular endurance, flexibility, and balance.

The U.S. policy was built on the goals pursued by the *Healthy People 2010: National Health Promotion and Disease Prevention Objectives* document (www.healthypeople.gov). This document sets forth 28 health objectives used by states, communities, professional organizations, and others to help develop programs to improve health and to enhance the quality and quantity of life for all citizens. The objectives are expansive and are not limited to improved childhood nutrition and increased physical activity; they are intended to increase understanding of and emphasis on health promotion and disease prevention while urging individuals to take on more personal responsibility to meet these goals.

The National Physical Activity Guidelines for Australians outlines minimum levels of physical activity required for attaining a health benefit and ways to incorporate incidental physical activity into everyday life.

The National Association for Sport and Physical Education (NASPE) and the American Heart Association recently endorsed the Fitness Integrated with Teaching Kids Act (FIT Kids Act) (H.R. 3257). On March 18, 2009, it was referred to the House Committee on Education and Labor. This federal legislation addresses the childhood obesity epidemic by putting more emphasis on increased physical education and physical activity for all schoolchildren across disciplines, and it suggests that physical activity be better integrated into the No Child Left Behind Act. On March 12, 2008, in Washington, D.C., American College of Sports Medicine (ACSM) president-elect Mindy Millard-Stafford led a Capitol Hill news conference with members of Congress to announce the introduction of a congressional bill to make the regular development and promotion of physical activity guidelines a reality. In the near future, we hope to see members of Congress calling on their colleagues to become cosponsors of this bill, the Physical Activity Guidelines for Americans Act. Although at this time it has not moved past Congress, the U.S. Department of Health and Human Services has issued its first-ever *Physical Activity Guidelines for Americans, 2008*, in which the types and amounts of physical activity that offer substantial health benefits to Americans have been outlined in four separate publications: one for policy makers and health professionals, one for adults ages 18 to 64, one for organizations and communities, and one for health professionals and researchers. In the U.K., the Change4Life program is a society-wide movement that aims to prevent people from becoming overweight by encouraging them to eat more healthfully and be more active. The Change4Life campaign began on January 3, 2009, in the press, on TV, on billboards, and online. In the initial stages, the movement targets young families.

The benefits of regular moderate-intensity physical activity have emerged as a worldwide issue as a result of the release of several key documents such as the ones mentioned here. The prevention of overweight and obesity in children, adolescents, and ultimately adults is the main objective. All of these federal programs and initiatives recommend involvement of parents, educators, administrators, counselors, and coaches in promoting healthy lifestyles so that children will have the skills to nourish their minds and bodies alike. All professionals who work with children are uniquely positioned to become elements of change and promoters of health and wellness. Good health is not something that just happens to people; it is something that people have a fair amount of control over. Health behaviors learned early can affect the health of an entire nation. *Healthy Breaks* is my response to this call to action.

This book supports the current emphasis on increased health promotion and disease prevention for youth. Anyone who works with children can offer these quick and easy activities to help students progress toward wellness and a healthy lifestyle. My experiences as a professor of health education and public school health and as a physical educator, coach, camp counselor, and staff developer have provided me with many opportunities to use these activities in a variety of settings and with diverse populations. All of these activities are designed for classrooms and small-space settings; access to gymnasiums is not necessary.

The activities promote health and wellness while creating a culture that infuses health literacy on a daily basis, whether in the classroom, at camp, or in after-school programs. Health literacy is the ability to think critically, solve problems, make decisions, and communicate effectively. Practicing these life skills will help to promote, sustain, and improve health. All of the activities include reference to the corresponding National Health Education Standards (NHES) that specify what the learners should know and be able to do. These standards support the knowledge and skills necessary for developing and maintaining health literacy. Activities also include reference to the National Association for Sport and Physical Education (NASPE) Standards, which support the knowledge and skill development for maintaining appropriate physical activity.

This book offers new and experienced professionals alike an opportunity to engage in exceptional teaching and student-centered learning experiences. Most activities take 5 to 10 minutes to prepare for. However, MapQuest; (Not) Seeing Is Believing; Stop, Drop, and Roll; and Stuck Like Glue Obstacle Course will take a little longer. Because of the minimal time involved in preparation and completion of activities, this book can be a tool for making every minute count. By simply modifying the equipment or one or two rules in any activity, you can introduce many variations to your students. Most of the activities are cooperative in nature with a modest competitive aspect. Participation for every child, not winning or losing, is a key element in *Healthy Breaks*. Teachers, program directors, after-school programmers, and camp counselors will discover new and exciting ways to promote health and wellness in a way that is exciting and conducive to improved classroom and group management.

Each activity in this book contains the following features in an easy-to-follow format:

- Aim is the purpose and rationale of the activity.
- Activity Objectives describe what the students will be able to do as a result of this activity.
- Grade Levels denote appropriate grade levels of participants.
- NHES Standards are the standards that guide the activity and define the learning objectives as they relate to health.
- NASPE Standards provide a framework for developing realistic and achievable expectations for students as they relate to physical activity.
- Suggested Time Requirements denote whether each activity is intended to be used within a 5-minute or 10-minute time frame.
- Materials Needed allow teachers to be prepared with the appropriate materials or equipment.
- Procedure describes the activity area, the step-by-step procedure for conducting the activity, how it is set up, and the rules.

- Safety Considerations suggest ways in which instructors can keep participants safe and free from injury.
- Tips and Variations offer suggestions on how the activity may be modified to enhance the experience.

These activities were first offered as an alternative to the traditional cupcake birthday party and holiday celebration. In the fall of 2005 I offered my own child's classroom teacher an opportunity to do something *different* for my son's birthday in the classroom. Instead of focusing the celebration on the food, I suggested minimizing that aspect and emphasizing the activity I was to present. This went over very well with students, faculty, and the attending class mothers. At the holiday celebration, once again I brought an activity to the party. I started a conversation with the school administrators in hopes of offering this to other classrooms; I was successful and was invited to offer a professional development experience at the district's kindergarten center. I have since offered this So Long, Cupcake! program to several area districts and presented the concept at several conferences regionally and nationally. The activities featured in *Healthy Breaks* are based on activities that I have used as a health and physical educator since 1990. I encourage you to say *so long, cupcake!* in your schools as well.

1

Quieting and Meditative Activities

School-age children undergo continual changes in every aspect of their lives. New experiences and unfamiliar routines are very often the primary sources of anxiety and stress. Children who are able to develop effective coping methods are more likely to manage the stressors of everyday life. These children tend to be happier and healthier as a result. Two of the tenets of coping skills are decision making and problem solving. Students as young as five years of age can learn a variety of coping skills that can evolve as they grow. When students learn the importance of daily physical activity, sound nutrition, socialization skills, and regular rest and sleep, they can develop a resiliency that can carry them throughout their lives.

Students in the lower grades (kindergarten to grade 2) can learn about stress and its effect on their bodies through teachable moments in the classroom, show-and-tell activities, and literacy activities. Young children can learn to differentiate good and bad bodily sensations and how those affect their emotions. Simple movement activities can induce playfulness and relaxation while increasing fitness. Older students (grades 3 to 6) can build on their basic understanding of stress and the differences between pleasant and unpleasant feelings. They can begin to develop a sense of awareness concerning the changes in their bodies as they experience stressful situations. With proper skill development, students will be empowered to not only identify the sources of stress but also realize that they can exert control over these situations. They can become their own agents of change and empowered to be responsible for their own health.

ALL ME: BODY AWARENESS

AIM
In this activity, students demonstrate and discuss feelings related to stress. Students will discuss how reactions to an event can influence your body (represented by a balloon). Students will also talk about how stressful feelings can build up in their bodies and cause harm if not expressed appropriately.

ACTIVITY OBJECTIVES
1. Students will be able to describe feelings related to stress.
2. Students will be able to identify causes of stress.
3. Students will be able to identify some ways they can reduce stressful feelings.
4. Students will be able to describe why it is important to manage stress effectively.

GRADE LEVELS   K-3

NHES STANDARDS   1, 2

NASPE STANDARDS   1, 2, 3

SUGGESTED TIME REQUIREMENTS   10 minutes

MATERIALS NEEDED
4 balloons: white, red, yellow, and green

PROCEDURE
1. Clear enough space so students can stand in a circle in the center of the classroom.

2. Discuss the concept of stress with the class before the activity commences. *Stress* can have many definitions; get a handle on what this means to you and what this may mean to your students. However, let me provide a generic definition of *stress* as I see it. *Stress* is the discomfort we feel when our lives are moving in direction A when we would rather be moving in direction B. Any variation of this would include demands made on us from ourselves, our families, our teachers, and our coaches. Knowing your population and making an assessment about the factors that may produce this discomfort are helpful (unstable family life, violence, overscheduling, homework).

Understanding the differences between good and bad feelings, where stress comes from, and what type of activities make participants feel better should be part of the discussion.

3. After this brief discussion, blow up the white balloon until it is very full and knot it. Pass the balloon around the circle and ask the children, "How do we need to handle the balloon?" (Here's an answer: Carefully, because it could pop.) Ask them what would happen if you put more air in it. (The balloon looks good and we could play with it and it would fun to bop it around. You or other students might suggest that too much air could make it more apt to burst during activity)

4. Take the red balloon and blow it up until it bursts. (Pop the balloon discreetly with a tack if you can't blow it up until it bursts.)

5. Ask the students why the balloon popped. Ask them, "Did I put too much air in it?" Discuss how air is like stress; if there is too much, the balloon breaks and can't be fixed.

6. Take the yellow balloon and blow some air in it. Do not tie the balloon. Ask students about what causes them to be stressed. With every answer, fill the balloon with another breath. After it is inflated, ask them what kinds of activities make them feel good and happy. With each answer, let some air out, demonstrating that they have some control over stress.

7. Let the balloon go and watch it go out of control. Ask students what may cause them to go out of control and discuss the appropriateness of this behavior. Perhaps discuss how they need to exert control over or manage their own stress so they don't go out of control.

8. Take the green balloon and blow it up to a point where it can be played with—not too much air, not too little air. The green balloon is a forgiving or resilient balloon. Ask the students how they can be more like the green balloon. (Suggested answers are exercise; play with friends; talk to their parents, teachers, and coaches.)

SAFETY CONSIDERATIONS

Ensure the safety of all students by pushing tables and chairs out of the way. Once the red balloon is broken, dispose of the pieces immediately so they do not pose a choking hazard. Latex allergies among children are infrequent but it's better to check this out beforehand.

TIPS AND VARIATIONS

You may ask students to identify which color balloon best represents them and why. You can ask them if they could change colors, which one it would be. Students can also draw pictures or write a story to further demonstrate their understanding.

I'M IN CONTROL

AIM

In this activity, students demonstrate that they have control over their reactions to stress and have a choice in the way they deal with the world and events around them.

ACTIVITY OBJECTIVES

1. Students will be able to describe feelings related to stress.
2. Students will be able to identify causes of stress in their own lives.
3. Students will be able to identify specific ways in which they can manage stress in their lives.

GRADE LEVELS   4-6

NHES STANDARDS   1, 2, 4

NASPE STANDARDS   6

SUGGESTED TIME REQUIREMENTS   10 minutes

MATERIALS NEEDED

1 small balloon for each student, 1 pen and 1 piece of paper for each group

PROCEDURE

1. Discuss the basic concept of stress with the class before the activity commences. *Stress* can have many definitions; get a handle on what this means to you and what this may mean to your students. However, let me provide a generic definition of *stress* as I see it. *Stress* is the discomfort we feel when our lives are moving in direction A when we would rather be moving in direction B. Any variation of this would include demands made on us from ourselves, our family, our teachers, and our coaches. Knowing your population and assessing the factors that may produce this discomfort is helpful (unstable family life, violence, overscheduling, homework). It is also important to understand the differences between good and bad feelings, where stress comes from, and what type of activities make them feel better.

2. Break up students into groups of three or four.

3. Tell them each group will have three lists and have them elect a recorder. The three lists are Physical Sensations While Stressed, Events That Have Caused Stress, and Techniques for Relieving Stress.

4. Have each member of the group identify a physical sensation they have experienced when feeling stressed; record the answers.

5. Ask the group to brainstorm and record a list of events that have caused stress for them lately. Here are examples: I forgot to bring my clarinet to school today. I left my homework on the kitchen table. My little brother hid the TV remote last night and no one can find it.

6. Have the students identify and record techniques that they have used to alleviate some of these sensations (take deep breaths, walk away, walk the dog, listen to music, ride your bike, talk to your mom).

7. Give each student a small balloon.

8. Go around the room and ask each group to provide two sensations from their first list. With each sensation that has been experienced, individual students are to blow once into their balloon. Have them hold the air in the balloon and do not tie the balloon.

9. Make references to the various sizes of balloons around the room. There will be different sizes of balloons because each student will have had different experiences and because each student will have blown different amounts of air into their balloons. It would be wise to note that at the start, every student has at least two breaths of air in their balloons; stress in one's life is universal.

10. Have students go around the room and have each group provide two or three events from the second list. Have all students blow into their balloons when they have shared the same experience.

11. Have students release air as you go around the room and identify ways in which some of the students have responded to or relieved stress. Some balloons may burst, and some may be very small. Have a few students summarize the exercise and guide them with questions such as these: What are some shared stressors? Why is something stressful for some and not others? How can we exert control over these feelings? Why are some people more successful in coping than others? (Answer is *resiliency*.) Why is it important to control these feelings?

SAFETY CONSIDERATIONS

Collect balloons before students leave the room because they may pose a choking hazard. Latex allergies among children are infrequent but it's better to check this out beforehand.

TIPS AND VARIATIONS

This activity can be followed up with additional questions. You may ask students to distinguish between inappropriate and appropriate responses to stress, or you may ask them to identify ways in which stress may lead to other feelings or emotions. Have students reflect or write in their journals about the experience for homework.

DEEP BREATHING

AIM

In this activity, students will learn how to quiet themselves and relieve tension. This deep-breathing technique is an ideal way to help students relieve stress, become quiet, and regain focus. This technique is easily learned and simple to perform, and it most often yields immediate pleasurable results. Deep breathing can be performed by anyone and can be done anywhere at any time. This makes deep breathing one of the most popular and convenient quieting and stress-relieving techniques.

ACTIVITY OBJECTIVES

1. Students will be able to identify the proper way to perform deep-breathing techniques.
2. Students will be able to perform deep-breathing techniques as a group and on their own.
3. Students will be able to learn to relax and de-stress, clearing the way for improved learning.
4. Students will be able to help create an environment where they can focus, learn, and perform successfully.
5. Students will be able to build self-esteem as they realize that they can contribute to their feelings of wellness and increase their potential.
6. Students will be able to link learning to health and wellness while addressing bodily-kinesthetic intelligence.

GRADE LEVELS   K-6

NHES STANDARDS   1, 4, 7

NASPE STANDARDS   6

SUGGESTED TIME REQUIREMENTS   10 minutes

MATERIALS NEEDED

None

PROCEDURE

1. Have students sit, stand, or lie down in a relaxed position.
2. Instruct students to close their eyes, inhale deeply through their mouths, and exhale *slowly* through their noses.

3. Instruct students to count to five to themselves as they inhale through their mouths and count to eight to themselves as they exhale through their noses. Instruct that they allow their abdomens to expand outward during the inhale as opposed to raising their shoulders. Emphasize that this should always be done slowly for best results. Repeat three times.

SAFETY CONSIDERATIONS

Students should sit or lie down on their first attempt because some students may become lightheaded. Do not exceed five attempts initially. Have students breathe in through the mouth and out through the nose to reduce the spread of germs as well as lengthen the exhale.

TIPS AND VARIATIONS

Have students assess themselves and verbally express how they feel immediately after their attempts. Depending on their knowledge of the human body, you may suggest that they imagine the air circulating and exchanging throughout their bodies (such as through the lungs, bronchioles, and alveoli) and drawing out tension, toxins, anxiety, and so on. This can be done very briefly within three minutes to instantly quiet students and relieve tension, stress, or anxiety.

MEDITATIVE BREATHING

AIM

Meditative breathing is an extension of the previous deep-breathing activity. Meditative breathing is a simple physical exercise that has both psychological and physical benefits. It can enhance personal peace of mind and increase self-confidence, self-efficacy, and academic efficiency while relieving physical tension. This technique may also assist students in regaining control over their emotions and provide opportunity for growth and empowerment. Like deep breathing, meditative breathing is also easily learned and simple to perform. Students will experience positive results initially and may yield increasing pleasurable results with practice.

In a classroom setting, this technique may be used for gaining control over emotions or feelings that prevent students from thinking rationally or behaving appropriately. These affective expressions may come in the form of anxiety, anger, jealousy, worry, and fear. Meditative breathing teaches students to calm their minds and subsequently free themselves of these expressions so they can think more clearly and behave more prosocially.

ACTIVITY OBJECTIVES

1. Students will be able to identify the proper way to perform meditative-breathing techniques.
2. Students will be able to perform meditative deep-breathing techniques as a group and on their own.
3. Students will be able to use this technique to increase peace of mind, self-confidence, self-efficacy, and academic efficiency while relieving physical tension.
4. Students will be able to learn to relax and de-stress, clearing the way for improved learning.
5. Students will be able to help create an environment where they can focus, learn, and perform successfully.
6. Students will be able to build self-esteem as they realize that they can contribute to their feelings of wellness and increase their potential.
7. Students will be able to link learning to health and wellness while addressing bodily-kinesthetic intelligence.

GRADE LEVELS K-6

NHES STANDARDS 1, 4, 7

NASPE STANDARDS 5, 6

SUGGESTED TIME REQUIREMENTS 10 minutes

MATERIALS NEEDED

Chairs; soothing music, perhaps classical or nature sounds; CD player

PROCEDURE

1. Have students sit in a relaxed position, preferably in a chair with a back. The chair should encourage students to sit upright and maintain good posture.

2. Have students sit upright with hands on their laps or resting on their desks.

3. Encourage students to relax their lower bodies with feet flat on the floor and legs uncrossed.

4. Tell students to close their eyes, inhale deeply through their mouths, and exhale *slowly* through their noses.

5. Tell students to count to five to themselves as they inhale through their mouths and count to eight to themselves as they exhale through their noses.

6. Tell them to allow their abdomens to expand outward as they inhale as opposed to raising their shoulders. Great emphasis should always be placed on the pace of this activity—*slowly* for best results. Once students seem to be relaxed, you may continue with the meditative portion.

7. For *quieting* and *enhancing personal peace of mind,* do the following: Have students choose a word to say to themselves, a word that evokes a positive feeling, such as *good, puppy, ice cream, summer, happy,* or *glorious.* Students choose their own words.

8. Tell students that they will repeat this word over and over as they sit silently and continue to breathe regularly. For young children I recommend one minute for each year of their age as they learn the procedure (for example, five minutes for a five-year-old). As they learn the procedure, they will happily sit and perform this technique longer. However, as a class you will often be limited by the attention span of your most fidgety student.

SAFETY CONSIDERATIONS

Students might need to sit in chairs rather than lie down; meditative breathing will not work if they fall asleep. Because blood pressure and heart rate often slow during this type of exercise, students' first movements should be placing their hands on the desks; do not allow them to rise quickly out of their seats because lightheadedness may occur. Have students breathe in through the mouth and out through the nose to reduce the spread of germs as well as lengthen the exhale.

TIPS AND VARIATIONS

Have students assess themselves either verbally or by writing in their journals about their experiences immediately after their attempts. Have students choose their word or phrase for the next time so that they are prepared for their next attempt, and encourage students to practice on their own and share the technique with their families.

Once they have the hang of it, you may want to introduce soothing music or nature sounds to enhance the experience. For enhancing self-confidence, self-efficacy, or academic performance, do the following: Have students choose a word or phrase themselves, a word or phrase that evokes a sense of empowerment instead of a positive feeling word as done in step 7, such as "I can . . .," "I will . . .," or "I am. . . ." Again, follow the minute-to-age ratio as suggested in step 8. When it is time to stop, give students a few moments to become adjusted to the normal routine. This experience also gets better with practice.

PROGRESSIVE MUSCLE RELAXATION

AIM

Even the youngest children can achieve relaxation by focusing their mental energies on this activity. This activity facilitates body awareness and may help redirect excess energy to a more positive position, the rewards of which can lead to peace of mind and an increased capacity for success and happiness in the daily lives of children.

ACTIVITY OBJECTIVES

1. Students will be able to implement the deep-breathing technique.
2. Students will be able to fully contract and relax specific muscle groups.
3. Students will be able to describe the steps necessary for performing progressive muscle relaxation.
4. Students will be able to describe how this activity can be used as a stress management technique.

GRADE LEVELS   K-6

NHES STANDARDS   1, 2, 7

NASPE STANDARDS   1, 2, 5, 6

SUGGESTED TIME REQUIREMENTS   10 minutes

MATERIALS NEEDED

Students may do this exercise in their seats or lying on the floor. If they will be on the floor, you may want to have them on a carpeted area or on beach towels or yoga mats.

PROCEDURE

1. Tell the children that they will be concentrating on relaxing all of the muscles in their bodies, one group at a time, in an ordered sequence.

2. This will be done by *tensing* (also known as *contracting*) the muscles in all the major groups: the head and neck, shoulders and chest, arms and hands, abdomen, back, buttocks, and legs and feet.

3. Depending on age of the children, you may have to go over what tensing and relaxing are and clarify the muscle groupings.

4. Have students lie on the floor or sit comfortably in chairs, away from each other.

5. Have students begin by taking one or two cleansing breaths as described in step 2 in the Deep Breathing activity, page 6.

6. Instruct them to close their eyes, focusing and listening to their own bodies.

7. Have them begin at the head, contracting the muscles in the face, jaw, and neck, holding this contraction for three to five seconds and releasing them in order to relax those muscles. Have them repeat this twice for each muscle group. When you have completed each muscle group, ask the students to take two cleansing breaths.

8. You may proceed with the following: shoulders, arms, hands, chest, back, abdomen, buttocks, legs, and feet.

9. Remind students to pay attention throughout these exercises so they will recognize how their muscles feel when they are tight and when they are relaxed.

10. Continue with this activity until you have covered all the muscles from the head to the feet.

11. Have them take a personal inventory of the sensations they are feeling.

SAFETY CONSIDERATIONS

Tell students that if they feel pain or cramping in any area of the body, they should stop immediately. If they feel physically uncomfortable during this activity, they can just lie there quietly and relax. Make sure students have enough room so that they won't touch each other during the activity.

TIPS AND VARIATIONS

You might want to use soothing music, such as classical music or nature sounds, to accompany this activity. You can follow up on this activity by suggesting that students can practice this almost anywhere. The best place to practice may be in their beds at night, where they can be quiet and undisturbed. Eventually, when they are really good at it they can do it whenever or wherever they need to.

VISUALIZATION ACTIVITY: AN ADVENTURE WITHIN

AIM

Visualization is yet another extension of the two previous activities. This technique is also called *guided imagery* by some. This technique uses the deep-breathing components in conjunction with relaxing scenes as described by you. By using a script, you describe a pleasant scene and allow the students to experience that scene as if they were there. Visualizing the relaxing scenes will translate into relaxation of the mind and relaxation of the body. This experience is largely self-generated; success is often dependent on the ability of the participant in using the mind's eye to get to the scene. Most children have little or no problem using their imaginations to visit these scenes. Children often relish this activity because of its autonomous nature. Visualization has both psychological and physical benefits because it equally relaxes and energizes while challenging students to take charge over their experience. By using various scripts, you can take students on imaginary field trips to the beach, the park, and the rain forest or for a quiet sail on a calm sunny lake, all while leaving them feeling at ease, clearing the way for improved learning and performance. The lesson is easy to use and lots of fun. This activity will assist you in linking learning to health, wellness, and self-responsibility.

ACTIVITY OBJECTIVES

1. Students will be able to perform visualization techniques as a group.
2. Students will be able to relax and clear the way for improved learning.
3. Students will be able to assist in creating an environment where they can focus, learn, and perform more successfully.
4. Students will be able to experience an increase in self-esteem as they realize they can contribute to their overall well-being.
5. Students will be able to link learning to health and wellness while addressing bodily-kinesthetic intelligence.

GRADE LEVELS 2-6

NHES STANDARDS 1, 6, 7, 8

NASPE STANDARDS   5, 6

SUGGESTED TIME REQUIREMENTS   10 minutes

MATERIALS NEEDED
Scripts or teacher's imagination, CD of nature sounds, and CD player

PROCEDURE

1. Students may sit in a relaxed position, preferably in a chair with a back, or may lie on the floor during this activity.

2. Encourage students to relax by employing a few deep breaths using the deep-breathing technique, close their eyes, and ready themselves for an adventure within their imaginations.

3. You set the scene by instructing the students that they may use their imagination freely, encouraging that they experience the scene in a variety of ways by seeing it, hearing it, smelling it, or feeling more peaceful for being there. You may use the following scripts or create one of your own.

4. When it is time to stop, give students a few moments to become adjusted to the normal routine.

THE BEACH

You may experience this scene as you like. You can imagine the scene any way you like. You are in control. Let your eyes remain relaxed as you imagine the following scene: You are standing on a quiet beach; feel the warm sun on your face and body. The sun feels good on your arms and legs and the warm sand feels nice through your toes. If the sun is too warm, there is a soft breeeze blowing to keep you feeling comfortable. The beach is beautiful, the water is calm, and you can see many families enjoying the sea and playing in the sand. As you stand there, you enjoy the warmth of the sun and the breeze. Slowly now, you walk along the beach enjoying the sand beneath your feet, the seagulls off in the distance, and the sounds of other children laughing as they play. The waves are small and you can hear the sound of the water as it brushes the sand at the water's edge. The smell of the salt air reminds you of a past visit to the beach with your family or friends. You look around and find a quiet spot on the beach away from other people. You spread out your beach blanket, put on your sunblock, and lie back ready to just relax. The warm sand feels good beneath you; you stretch your arms and legs as you lie there, allowing the sand to warm your body. You feel the bright sun on your face and it makes you feel relieved and comfortable. Everything around you seems bright and happy and warm. As you lie there on the blanket, the sun seems to be warming your face and then your chest and arms. As you stretch out, your feet dig small holes in the sand; you can feel the damp coolness on your toes. The sun warms your belly and your legs; you feel great. Your muscles are relaxed and you feel as though the sand is as comfortable as your bed. Your body feels heavy and warm, you take a deep breath to smell the salt air, and as you exhale you feel light and peaceful. You look up and you see the seagulls flying so free and easy you imagine them carrying away all your worries and problems. You are totally relaxed and feel happy to have had such a wonderful day. You can think of nothing better than the blue sky above and the gentle waves of the ocean. As you take another deep breath, you feel as if you have woken from a beautiful dream. You now realize that the sun is fading and it is time to head home. As you slowly sit up on the blanket, you look around so that you can remember this beautiful day forever. You look at the birds flying and the other people getting ready to also leave the beach. You take one last deep breath as you stretch your arms and legs and get ready to pack up and head home. After you pack up your blanket, you walk slowly down the beach feeling the now-cooled sand beneath your feet. You have enjoyed your time alone on the beach, and you feel relaxed and happy to leave. You know you can visit that beach again whenever you want.

THE WOODS

You are walking on a dirt path in the middle of the day. It is very sunny and you feel the sun warming your face and your shoulders as you walk toward the edge of a wooded area. As you near the edge of the woods, you walk along a small flowing stream. You stop and look at the stream; the water is perfectly clear and sounds like water running from a hose. You bend down and touch the water; it is cool and fresh. You look around at the trees and bushes that grow near the stream; everything is a rich green color and you hear a gentle breeze as it blows through the trees and the nearby woods. As the wind blows and the breeze comes toward you, you smell the pine cones and sweet smell of fallen leaves. You cross over the small stream and head into the woods. As you look up, you can see the strong sun pouring through the treetops. You can hear birds singing and see squirrels running up and down the branches above you. You feel safe and secure in this beautiful place. You take a deep breath inward and feel as though you have been energized by all the beauty around you. You hear the faint sounds of running water and you see a large rock and stop to sit on it; it is cool and damp beneath you.

(continued)

As you sit, you lean over and see that just beneath you is a small waterfall that flows into a small pool of calm water. In that small pool you can see tiny fish flickering about as if they are playing tag with one another. The breeze sends leaves floating in the air; as they gently fall to the ground, you feel peaceful and allow yourself to relax. As you sit there you spot several birds flying effortlessly back and forth. You imagine you are one of those birds gliding and drifting with the wind; you feel free and as light as a feather. You take a deep breath and feel your body relaxing as it is warmed by the sunlight. You decide it is time to return to the road. As you get up to leave that peaceful place, you step on tiny twigs and hear them crackle beneath your feet. As you slowly walk to the stream, you spot a deer taking a drink of water; both you and the deer seem to look directly at each other. As you stand silently, the deer slowly trots off in the other direction. You continue to walk up the dirt path; you again feel the direct sun on your face and shoulders. You may visit these woods again whenever you want to feel safe and relaxed.

YOUR SPECIAL PLACE

You find yourself in the one place where you always feel safe, warm, and comfortable. This might be on your favorite chair or couch or even in your bed at night. Wherever this may be, picture yourself in your special place; you are feeling happy and safe. You are looking forward to a few minutes alone—not too far from your loved ones but far enough so that you can relax by yourself. As you sit or lie in your special place, you cozy up with your favorite blanket, pillow, or stuffed animal. That cozy blanket or pillow is yours and yours alone. There is nowhere else that you would rather be at this moment. You can hear the sounds of the street and the traffic moving along. The sounds are muffled by the rumblings of a nearby subway train or bus, or by the television in the next room; these are the sounds of your special place. You close your eyes and in your mind's eye you can see this special place, with you in it, just the way you like it. As you take a deep breath, you feel the softness of that pillow beneath your head and the stuffed toy in your arms. You can faintly smell your favorite food cooking in the kitchen. As you smell the familiar aromas, you remember the many times you have sat or lain in this place feeling good, feeling happy, and feeling warm. Take this moment to remember the last time you were in this special place. Remember how good it felt to be there and remember the things that make this place so special to you. This place may have some of your prized possessions there: your pet, your toys, your books, and the people you love. Imagine that you are there and all of your stuff is right where you want it to be and all the people you care about are right where you want them to be.

In this place you can be exactly who you want to be: You can be noisy, you can be silly, you can be sleepy, or you can be quiet or sad. This is your place, and you are comfortable there. Take a deep breath, and in your mind's eye take a look at that place with you in it, looking good, and smell the aromas around you and hear the familiar noise from the neighborhood. You feel warm, you feel relaxed, and you feel safe. You can visit this special place any time you want.

SAFETY CONSIDERATIONS

Instruct students to slowly sit up at first, giving them space to reorient themselves to the present. Ask them to return to their seats only when they have acclimated to their environment.

TIPS AND VARIATIONS

Have students assess themselves either verbally or by writing in their journals about their experiences immediately after their attempts. You may also allow them to draw or use watercolors to express their experience. Ask students where they would like to go next time—perhaps the park or the woods for a scenic hike along a pond. Again, once they have the hang of it, you may want to introduce soothing music or nature sounds to enhance the experience. This experience also gets better with practice.

BREATHING, VISUALIZATION, AND EMOTIONAL EXPRESSION

AIM

We know that children of all ages feel the effects of overstimulation, overscheduling, and stress. Most often they do not understand these feelings, are unable to express these feelings, and are ill-equipped to cope. Thus, the aim of this activity is twofold: first, to help young learners identify when they are overburdened or stressed and, second, to teach them simple techniques to cope with their emotions. By integrating simple breathing techniques, visualization, and novel ways of expressing themselves, students and teachers alike will enjoy some quiet time in the classroom. This activity will assist you in linking learning to health, wellness, and self-responsibility.

ACTIVITY OBJECTIVES

1. Students will be able to identify what stress is and how it affects their lives.
2. Students will be able to identify particular coping methods (breathing, visualization, artistic expression).
3. Students will experience an increase in self-esteem as they realize they can contribute to their overall well-being.

GRADE LEVELS   2-6

NHES STANDARDS   1, 2, 4, 7, 8

NASPE STANDARDS   5, 6

SUGGESTED TIME REQUIREMENTS   10 minutes

MATERIALS NEEDED

Watercolor trays, water, brushes, and paper for each student; newsprint to absorb accidental spills; scripts; CD of nature sounds or classical music; CD player

PROCEDURE

1. The basic concept of stress is discussed with the class before the activity commences. *Stress* can have many definitions; get a handle on what this means to you and what this may mean to your students. However, let me provide a generic definition of *stress* as I see it. *Stress*

is the discomfort we feel when our lives are moving in direction A when we would rather be moving in direction B. Any variation of this would include demands made on us from ourselves, our families, our teachers, and our coaches. Knowing your population and making an assessment about the factors that may produce this discomfort are helpful (unstable family life, being bullied, soccer practice, music lessons, homework).

2. You discuss stress and how it may apply to the lives of the students; you have a brief discussion about how this may make the students feel. Reassure them that these feelings are legitimate and likely shared by their peers.

3. You may want to put up a list of these feelings (that is, brainstorm) on the board so the children can access them for the activity.

4. Instruct the children that they should use the paints to express what they are feeling when they are stressed. For example, a young child may say that he has too many soccer practices or too much homework. Encourage them to paint freely, perhaps using colors, words, or pictures to represent their feelings. You will see that this activity takes on a life of its own quickly.

5. You can further develop this activity by asking them how they handle these situations, and perhaps how their caregivers handle them. You may help them make the connection between the events in their lives and how they feel and ultimately how those factors make them act or behave. Younger students may not have the dialogue for this but they absolutely are able to understand the concept.

6. At this point you may offer the coping methods they have previously learned with deep breathing, visualization, or meditation. Have them practice the breathing methods, and then ask them to express with paint how that makes them feel.

7. Repeat with the visualization or meditation techniques, and then have them express themselves with paint.

8. Experiment with the nature sounds or classical music and allow them to paint. The goal is to get students to notice the difference between feelings of stress and feelings of relaxation.

9. Emphasize the following: Stress is part of everyday life and is not going away; they have influence over how they feel; and they need to communicate these feelings to their caregivers, teachers, and coaches.

SAFETY CONSIDERATIONS

This activity easily accommodates many students. Watercolor paints are used because they do not stain clothing and are very easy to work with. Watercolor trays are inexpensive and can be used by more than one student at a time.

TIPS AND VARIATIONS

Depending on the age of the students, you may have them write in their journals about their experiences immediately after their attempts.

Esteem Builders

C hildren of all ages need praise and appreciation and thrive on positive attention. Words of encouragement raise children's spirits, confidence, performance, and self-esteem. Self-esteem is often an indicator of a person's mental health and can be nurtured; next to parents, teachers, counselors, and coaches, self-esteem plays an equally vital role in this form of health promotion. Helping children develop confidence and feel good about themselves is a responsibility that can be easily achieved. Giving children the opportunity to act independently from adults and cooperatively with their peers provides unique opportunities for growth and development. Providing children with novel experiences and requiring them to assume responsibility and express independence in thought and expression in a safe and fun way help them develop life skills that bolster confidence. These activities provide experiences that allow children to share their thoughts, emotions, and unique qualities. Participation in these activities enhances development of social skills and self-concept.

ABCS AND ME (ATTITUDES, BEHAVIORS, CONSEQUENCES)

AIM

This activity illustrates that we have control over our behaviors and actions as well as our thoughts and feelings. These thoughts and feelings influence our attitudes and behaviors. Unfortunately, the consequences of these behaviors are not always in our control because we cannot predict how others will respond to our behaviors.

ACTIVITY OBJECTIVES

1. Students will be able to demonstrate that they understand they can control their behaviors.
2. Students will be able to verbalize their understanding of the attitudes, behaviors, and consequences sequence.
3. Students will be able to verbalize which of the following they have the greatest control over—attitudes, behaviors, or consequences.

GRADE LEVELS   2-6

NHES STANDARDS   1, 2, 5, 6

NASPE STANDARDS   1, 2, 5, 6

SUGGESTED TIME REQUIREMENTS   10 minutes

MATERIALS NEEDED

Three like-sized differently colored balls, each labeled A, B, or C (small kickballs work well); music for "Hot Potato," and a CD player

PROCEDURE

1. Make an open space in the classroom and have children sit or stand in the center of the room in a large circle.

2. Place the marked balls in the center. Each ball is marked A, B, or C.

3. Tell them that *A* represents *attitudes,* *B* represents *behaviors,* and *C* represents *consequences.* Explain these terms to younger children.

4. One at a time, pass the A ball around quickly like a "hot potato." When you stop the music, the child with the ball has to hold it and give an example of an attitude (for example, an attitude about vegetables,

bedtime, or teeth brushing); the responses can be positive or negative, such as "I love broccoli" or "I hate brushing my teeth."

5. Once you are certain that everyone understands attitudes, move on to the B ball. Pass around the ball and when the music stops, ask them for behaviors (for example, what they do when their parents tell them to go to bed).

6. Pass around the C ball and ask for consequences of any of the topics discussed with the other two balls. Some students may get the connection and others may not.

7. Put the A, B, and C balls in a line, perhaps on a desk for a more dramatic effect, and push the A ball into the B ball and so on.

8. Have students suggest the connection among attitudes, behaviors, and consequences.

9. Ask the students which they have the best control over, attitudes, behaviors, or consequences. Why is it important to consider the consequences before choosing a behavior? (A suggested answer is that if someone's attitude about eating vegetables is negative, this will prompt negative behavior. If he or she won't eat a vegetable or carries on about eating it, the consequences may be an angry parent or punishment.)

SAFETY CONSIDERATIONS

Move all the desks aside to provide the most room. You could ask a student to handle the music portion. When you are done with the A and B balls, secure them so no one falls over them, and they don't create a temptation.

TIPS AND VARIATIONS

If you want to infuse more energy into the activity, allow students to bounce the ball across the circle to one another. If less activity is required, have students sit and pass.

I FEEL GOOD, YOU FEEL GOOD

AIM

In this activity, students give and receive compliments from one another and demonstrate their ability to use interpersonal communication to enhance their health and the health of others.

ACTIVITY OBJECTIVES

1. Students will be able to work as group.
2. Students will be able to state their feelings toward others around them.
3. Students will be able to express their own feelings of identity or mastery to others in the group.

GRADE LEVELS 1-6

NHES STANDARDS 1, 2, 4

NASPE STANDARDS 5, 6

SUGGESTED TIME REQUIREMENTS 10 minutes

MATERIALS NEEDED

Before the activity begins, cut strips of paper measuring 1 inch by 11 inches from different-colored construction paper. Cut enough strips so that each student gets six strips of paper. Each group of students will need cellophane tape and some markers.

PROCEDURE

1. Have students break up into groups of five or six.

2. Have them arrange their chairs so that they are facing each other or have them sit on the floor.

3. Each student in the group takes a strip of paper, puts his or her name on it, and makes a loop. Use the tape to secure the ends.

4. Individual students pass the loop with their name on it to the person next them.

5. That student takes an unused strip and writes something positive about the person whose loop they have. Then it is passed to the next person.

6. Loop all the comments together, and eventually each individual will have a small chain of positive comments about himself or herself.

7. At this point, the owner of the chain writes something positive about herself or himself and attaches it to the last loop.

8. Once everyone has a completed chain, give students a few minutes to get up and go around the room and find someone else with whom they share a common attribute; they can link their loops together.

9. If time permits, allow students to link several chains together and eventually they all will be connected. This can be displayed in the room as a reminder of the positive effect this exercise had on the participants.

10. As this is occurring, you can ask students to comment about how the exercise made them feel. Was it easy or difficult to make positive comments about others in the classroom? How much of what people say influences the way we feel? How can we be responsible to others by maintaining a positive atmosphere?

SAFETY CONSIDERATIONS

None.

TIPS AND VARIATIONS

Younger children may need help with spelling, so you might brainstorm a list of possible comments on the board so they can copy entire phrases. You may want to have students write a positive comment about themselves only. When everyone has done this, tell them to go around the room and find another person with whom they have something in common, and then have these individuals link their strips together. After everyone is linked to at least one other person, you can facilitate a discussion that links all the groups together, hopefully leading to one happy family of individuals with both common and unique interests.

A DIFFERENT VIEW

AIM

In this activity, students evaluate and compare different ways of viewing the world around them, which helps them realize how communication with others can be useful and gratifying during times of need. Additionally, students also see that it is possible to turn a negative into a positive with help and a different perspective.

ACTIVITY OBJECTIVES

1. Students will be able to describe the utility and power of communication.

2. Students will be able to explain the concept of *perspective*.

3. Students will be able to describe how one can use a different perspective to see the good in a negative experience.

4. Students will be able to list ways in which they can use the skills of perception and communication as stress management techniques.

5. Students will be able to differentiate feelings of sadness, anger, happiness, or fear.

6. Students will be able to appropriately express their feelings.

GRADE LEVELS   2-6

NHES STANDARDS   1, 2, 4, 7

NASPE STANDARDS   5, 6

SUGGESTED TIME REQUIREMENTS   10 minutes

MATERIALS NEEDED

Poster board, one piece for each group; several crayons or markers for each student to use within their groups

PROCEDURE

1. After putting students into groups of four, arrange the desks in a square so that all desks face each other, or push the desks aside and have students sit on the floor. Give each group one sheet of poster board.

2. Tell one student to divide the poster board into four equal quadrants.

3. Each student writes his or her name in the corner of the closest quadrant.

4. Have one member of the group be the recorder.

5. Tell the students to brainstorm a list of events that cause stress (such as failing a test, breaking up with a boyfriend or girlfriend, losing a soccer game, not having a play date, and so on) and have the recorder write the events on the back of the poster board.

6. Once they have the list, ask students to think about a time when they felt stressed over one of those experiences. Encourage them use their mind's eye to relive the event.

7. Have them turn the poster board over and write the feeling that accompanied that event (for example, angry, sad, embarrassed, disrespected, or lonely) in the quadrant under their names.

8. Tell students to scribble in their spaces to relieve some of those stressful feelings.

9. After about one minute, tell the students to turn the paper clockwise so that they have another student's square in front of them.

10. The job is now twofold: First, have each student add a word or short phrase to help change the owner's perception of the event; second, have students make the scribble into something nice.

11. Every two minutes or so, turn the paper clockwise to allow the next person to add a comment and add to this picture.

12. Continue until the quadrants make it back to the original owners.

13. You may assess the activity in the following ways:

- Have the students look at the comments from their classmates and see what the scribble turned into.
- Ask the students what the purpose of this activity was.
- Ask the students what stress management techniques were applied in this activity (some possible answers are communication, humor, altering of perception, relaxation in the drawing activity, or reaching out to others for assistance).
- Ask the students how this activity made them feel. What did they realize as result of this exercise?

SAFETY CONSIDERATIONS

Use washable markers. Smaller children may not be able to reach the poster board in the center of the desks, so you might want to have them sit on the floor for this activity. If so, make sure the desks are out of the way so that students will have enough space to pass the paper around and be comfortable.

TIPS AND VARIATIONS

Instead of turning the paper clockwise within the group, you might have them pass the entire poster board to the next group and allow each person to pick a quadrant and add to the picture. Continue passing the poster board around until it gets back to the original group and owner.

WHO AM I?

AIM
This activity promotes emotional health and enhances children's social skills development and self-concept. This is done in a way that relies on recognition from their peers, which best represents true achievement because it is defined by their contemporaries. Students lend support to each other by identifying others' unique attributes and contributions.

ACTIVITY OBJECTIVES
1. Students will be able to explain the concept of *uniqueness*.
2. Students will be able to recognize their own unique contributions as well as the contributions of their peers.
3. Students will be able to give and receive compliments from their peers.
4. Students will be able to demonstrate that they value and respect each other.

GRADE LEVELS   3-6

NHES STANDARDS   1, 4

NASPE STANDARDS   5, 6

SUGGESTED TIME REQUIREMENTS   5-10 minutes

MATERIALS NEEDED
One sheet of blank 8.5-by-11-inch paper, a piece of tape, and one washable marker for each student.

PROCEDURE
1. Before you begin, discuss the concept of individual *uniqueness* and why it is important in understanding who we are and how others see us. You can also elicit some examples of positive contributions students have made in the school, community, home, camp, or environment.

2. Have students tape the paper to the back of a fellow classmate.

3. Ask students to walk around the room and allow other students to write a thoughtful comment on the paper. The comments should be positive and refer to the uniqueness or the special contributions that individual brings to the community. Here are some examples:

You are always smiling. You are a leader. You are always happy. You are helpful and kind. You are good in math. You are a good sport. It is essential to emphasize that the comments be thoughtful and positive so that everyone walks away empowered by this activity. Allow this to continue until everyone has written on everyone else's paper or set a certain number of comments.

SAFETY CONSIDERATIONS

You must emphasize that the comments need to be positive and should focus on the positive contributions of the individual, not just material possessions. Remind students that this is a serious exercise and unacceptable comments will not be tolerated. Using washable markers prevents staining of clothing.

TIPS AND VARIATIONS

You may want to further process this activity with a literacy exercise. Students can write a reaction to or reflection of the experience, and you might guide them with questions. Here are some possible questions: How do you feel about the comments made about you? How did it make you feel focusing on the positive contributions of your peers? How did you feel about sharing these feelings with your peers? Have your perceptions of self been challenged by this experience?

THE QUALITIES OF ME! (PART 1)

AIM
This activity allows students to think about friendships and the qualities that make a good friend. Students identify the positive qualities they espouse and are looking for in a friend.

ACTIVITY OBJECTIVES
1. Students will be able to explain the importance of friendship and how friendships can influence a person's health.
2. Students will be able to identify the qualities that make a good friend.
3. Students will be able to identify the positive qualities they uniquely espouse.

GRADE LEVELS   3-4

NHES STANDARDS   1, 2, 3

NASPE STANDARDS   5

SUGGESTED TIME REQUIREMENTS   10 minutes

MATERIALS NEEDED
One sheet of paper for each student and several crayons or markers for students to share

PROCEDURE
1. While seated at their desks, ask the students why friendships are important to our health. Write this list on the board (some possible answers are to be happy, to rely on each other, to care for one another, or to help one another).

2. Ask students what qualities are important in a friend and write the responses on the board (suggested answers are loyalty, kindness, helpfulness, understanding).

3. Briefly examine these with the class to ensure understanding.

4. Ask students to create a personal advertisement that identifies one of their good qualities. They can draw a picture and use words to advertise their quality. These should remain anonymous.

5. When everyone has completed their advertisements, they can be displayed on the board or on the desks.

6. Students will now have the opportunity to "shop" for a friend based on the qualities they are looking for. When they find an ad they like, they should write their names on the bottom of the advertisement.

7. When this is complete, all ads will have names on them.

8. Close with the idea that everyone has positive qualities and is worthy of friendships, and sometimes people need to look past the obvious to see what matters the most.

SAFETY CONSIDERATIONS

It is important to moderate this activity so that everyone walks away feeling good. You might want to participate to ensure that every advertisement is signed; most often, other students will follow your lead.

TIPS AND VARIATIONS

You may want to allow students to identify their ads, which might open the door for new friendships. Ahead of time you could clip pictures or words from magazines for students to apply to their ads, which might help students with little artistic initiative. Use this activity as a precursor to the Good Friend Wanted activity that follows.

▶ An advertisement created by a student.

THE QUALITIES OF ME! (PART 2): GOOD FRIEND WANTED

AIM

This activity assists students in identifying, recognizing, and developing healthy positive relationships among their peers.

ACTIVITY OBJECTIVES

1. Students will be able to explain the importance of friendship and how friendships can influence health.
2. Students will be able to identify the qualities that make a good friend.
3. Students will be able to identify the qualities they look for in a friend.
4. Students will be able to select a new friend from the advertisements and have the opportunity to meet this new friend.

GRADE LEVELS   3-4

NHES STANDARDS   1, 2, 3

NASPE STANDARDS   5

SUGGESTED TIME REQUIREMENTS   10 minutes

MATERIALS NEEDED

One sheet of paper for each student and several crayons or markers for students to share; completed advertisements from part 1 of this activity

PROCEDURE

1. While students are at their desks, brainstorm with the students and discuss the qualities that they believe are the most desirable in a good friend.

2. Ask each student to create a list of the qualities they are looking for in a new friend.

3. All students must write down at least five qualities they are looking for in a friend.

4. Once everyone has a list, the students can "shop" for a new friend using the advertisements created in the previous activity.

5. Allow students to peruse the ads and select one. Have students bring this ad back to their seats and discuss in small groups the reason they chose that particular advertisement.

6. You may choose to have students identify which ads are theirs, possibly sparking some new relationships among the group.

SAFETY CONSIDERATIONS

It is important to moderate this activity so that everyone walks away feeling good. You might want to participate so that every advertisement is chosen; most often, other students will follow your lead.

TIPS AND VARIATIONS

If you do not want to piggyback this activity with The Qualities of Me! (Part 1) activity, you could have students create want ads for a good friend. Have them identify the quality or qualities they are looking for and post their ads in the room. Have students create these anonymously and allow space at the bottom for interested parties to apply. At the end of the day, you can collect the want ads and return them to their owners—they may have a potential new friend among the group. Encourage students to reach out to these new friends. You might want to develop a parent letter discussing this activity to achieve their support beforehand.

▶ An advertisement created by a student that lists the qualities most desirable in a good friend.

Social Wellness Activities

The activities in this chapter have been chosen because they have been field-tested and proven to be successful in getting children to share, cooperate, and have fun. These activities allow students to practice these skills and experience their value. Given the opportunity to fine-tune these skills, children come away with an increased respect for themselves and others, a sincere sense of caring, a heightened admiration for one another, and the strengthened ability to interact in a prosocial and healthy way. Sharing activities reflect the realities of the communities we live in. When conflict arises in our lives, it is most often the result of a lack of caring, respect, shared responsibility, and competent communication. The advantage of these games is that no one is left out, there are no losers, and children are directed to play with one another and not against one another. These activities eliminate feelings of alienation and failure and foster emotional and social wellness among the group. Similar to the activities in chapter 2, these also promote self-esteem and self-confidence. These activities focus on self-discovery, mutual understanding, patience, and challenge, and result in group success. All of these qualities are well-suited for providing young people with ample opportunity for increased health and wellness on many levels. Sharing is a life skill that we depend on to get along in the world around us. Learning how to share and cooperate early in life absolutely enhances the ability to succeed. Working toward a shared vision or expected outcome affords every child a chance to contribute and experience a win.

BALLOON BOUNCE

AIM
This activity reinforces the idea of sharing and working toward a common goal.

ACTIVITY OBJECTIVES
1. Students will be able to have fun and experience success in the activity while sharing the equipment.
2. Students will be able to identify the importance of taking turns.
3. Students will be able to verbalize the importance of communication among team members.

GRADE LEVELS   K-3

NHES STANDARDS   1, 4, 5, 6, 7

NASPE STANDARDS   1, 2, 5, 6

SUGGESTED TIME REQUIREMENTS   5-10 minutes

MATERIALS NEEDED
One balloon for every three students. Have extras blown up in case one breaks during the activity. Oversized round balloons work best because they move the slowest and float well. One hula hoop for each group.

PROCEDURE
1. Have children make groups of three or four and spread out throughout the room. Move desks out of the way so students have an open playing space.
2. Tell them they will have to share a balloon among the group (they may complain at first but that is what you want).
3. Tell them that their first goal is to see if they can have fun sharing one balloon among three people.
4. Challenge them to bump the balloon around the group so that everyone touches the balloon before it hits the floor.
5. If they are successful, have them predict how many consecutive bumps they can achieve before the balloon hits the floor.
6. Congratulate their efforts and achievements.

7. Further challenge them by adding another piece of equipment, a hula hoop. Tell the students to bump or throw the balloon through the hoop.

8. One student holds the hoop over his or her head (if you are working with a group of four, have two children hold the hoop) while the other two take turns passing the ball through the hoop. Continue as time permits.

SAFETY CONSIDERATIONS

Ensure that the desks or chairs are cleared away so that the children can move about safely. Do not allow children to blow up the balloons and dispose of any broken balloons immediately so there is not a choking hazard.

TIPS AND VARIATIONS

To process this activity, you might talk about how much fun they had sharing and ask them what it was like to take turns and what role communication played in their fun.

This activity can be done as a timed event; for example, how many passes through the hoop can they achieve? How many bumps in one minute? How many different body parts can they use in one minute? Older children (grades 4 through 6) can be challenged to play in groups of four. Two students hold the hoop above their heads while the other two face each other on either side of the hoop. You can challenge the students to hit the balloon through the hoop and then rotate around the hoop before the balloon hits the floor.

STUCK LIKE GLUE OBSTACLE COURSE

AIM
This activity promotes the concepts of sharing, communication, and working toward a common goal.

ACTIVITY OBJECTIVES
1. Students will be able to have fun and experience success in the activity while sharing the equipment.
2. Students will be able to identify the importance of taking turns.
3. Students will be able to verbalize the importance of communication between team members.

GRADE LEVELS   4-6

NHES STANDARDS   1, 4, 5, 6, 7

NASPE STANDARDS   1, 2, 5, 6

SUGGESTED TIME REQUIREMENTS   15 minutes

MATERIALS NEEDED
One balloon for each pair of students; eight cones; two chairs; four hula hoops; two hockey sticks or meter sticks; and two jump ropes

PROCEDURE
1. Move all of the chairs and desks away from the center of the room.

2. Using the cones, hoops, chairs, and jump ropes, set up an obstacle course as stations around the room; spread out the stations as much as space will allow. Use the cones for students to weave through or to go around, upright chairs to sit on or downed chairs to walk over, the hockey sticks to create two hurdles, and the jump ropes for a limbo station (see diagram, page 39).

3. Team up two children and give each team a balloon. The object of this activity is to have the students use the balloon as if it were glue, binding the two together. Students try to keep the balloon between their bodies without using their hands.

4. Students go through the obstacles stuck together.

5. If they drop the balloon, they can simply replace it between their bodies. All of the students will have fun, and they will all feel like winners.

SAFETY CONSIDERATIONS

This activity is difficult so expect that the pace will be slow. Make sure that the course is free from objects that could pose a safety threat. Have extra blown-up balloons handy in case one bursts. Keep in mind that the height of the hurdles should be only as high as your shortest participant can manage.

TIPS AND VARIATIONS

For smaller groups you can have teams start at one of the stations and have them complete the obstacle course in circuit fashion, ending when they are back to where they started. For larger classes you can start one team at a time; as soon as the first teams gets through the first obstacle, send the next team. Once a team finishes, have them sit back to back, with the balloon between them, in the center of the class. To further process this activity, you could talk about how much fun they had sharing responsibilities and ask why they were successful and what role communication played in this activity and their fun.

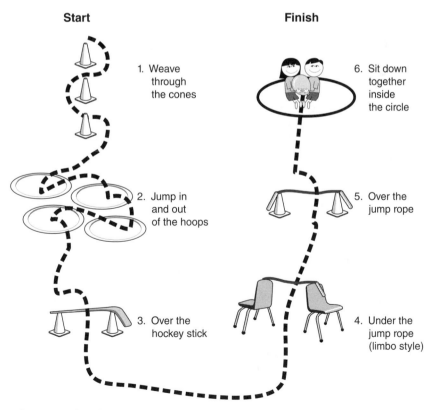

▶ Suggested obstacle course setup.

THE CURIOUS SNAIL

AIM

This activity requires a group of students to move cooperatively from one place to another and perform tasks as a group. Students share responsibility in decision making to complete these tasks.

ACTIVITY OBJECTIVES

1. Students will be able to move around as a group.
2. Students will be able to complete a task as a group by collectively making decisions.
3. Students will be able to recognize that sometimes it is okay to slow down and think about their actions before they take action.

GRADE LEVELS   3-6

NHES STANDARDS   1, 3, 5, 6, 7

NASPE STANDARDS   1, 2, 5, 6

SUGGESTED TIME REQUIREMENTS   10 minutes

MATERIALS NEEDED

A twin- or queen-size fitted bedsheet (one with elastic trim all the way around) for every group ("snail"); cutouts or plastic toy food choices, some healthy and some unhealthy (enough cutouts to allow at least one per student); alphabet cutouts or the small refrigerator-magnet type (about five A-Z sets per "snail"); one hula hoop for every group ("snail")

PROCEDURE

1. Discuss how a snail moves slowly and deliberately.

2. Put children in groups of five or six and give each group a fitted sheet.

3. Children get in a circle and drop to their hands and knees, with faces outward and feet toward the middle.

4. Place the fitted sheet over their heads so that the elastic goes around the forehead area.

5. Challenge the children to move about as a unified group. The tasks should start out simply and become more complex as the students get the knack of moving about.

6. Start simply; first by asking the snail to move (on hands and knees) to a fixed position, then have the snail turn in a circle, and finally have the snail go left or right on command. Once this is accomplished, you may move on to tasks. For example, ask the snail what all living things need in order to be healthy (the answers are food, water, sleep, and shelter).

7. Have the snails start out from their "nests" (the four corners of the room can be used). Place a hula hoop on the floor to represent the nest; this is also used as a place to deposit the food (see diagram, page 42).

8. Send the snail to the "store" (located in the center of the room) to select a healthy meal for itself or its human owner using the food cutouts or toys. Make sure that before the snail returns to its nest, it has discussed and decided as a group which items are the best choices to keep humans or snails healthy.

9. When the snail needs to make a decision, it can retract beneath its shell to decide. Students can sit cross-legged and face the center to discuss and decide.

10. When they are through with the discussion, have students place the selected food items on top of the shell (on top of the sheet) and work cooperatively to bring the meal home.

11. When it is time to return to the nest, the students face outward again and move as a group.

12. Place the alphabet letters in the center of the room. This is now called the "library."

13. Ask students any health-related question you like, such as "How many hours of sleep do young humans need?" or "What type of foods should humans eat the least?" Ask questions one at a time, after which you allow the snail to creep over to the library and retrieve the alphabet letters necessary for spelling out their answers. The letters are brought back to the nest on top of the shell and the answers spelled out within the hoop. Continue as time allows.

SAFETY CONSIDERATIONS

Make sure the activity area is clear. The snail shell (fitted sheet) should not cover the faces of the students. Advise students when they retract within the shell to do so slowly so that no one bumps heads. When moving from place to place, the students should move as a snail does—*slowly,* going only as fast as the slowest member of the group.

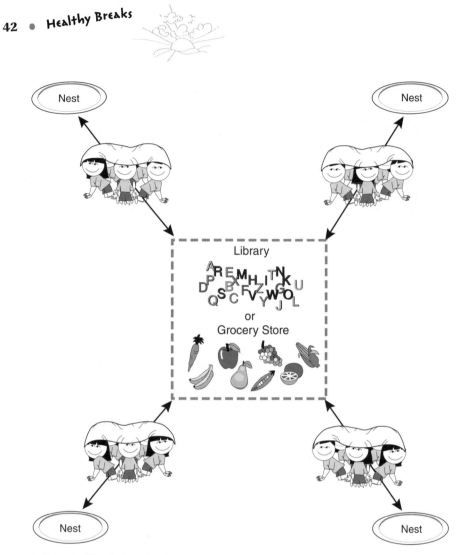

▶ Setup for The Curious Snail.

TIPS AND VARIATIONS

As students get better working together, you can make the tasks more difficult, either intellectually or physically. If you have a large class you can have two or more snails; you can change the size of the fitted sheet to accommodate the number and size of participants. Bigger children will need more room beneath the sheet and smaller children need less. Younger children (kindergarten through grade 2) can fit five or six beneath a twin-fitted sheet. Older students (grades 3-6) may only be able to fit three or four students beneath a twin sheet; use a queen-size sheet to accommodate more students.

THE HUNGRY SNAKE

AIM

This activity allows students to share equipment and understand the responsibilities of decision making and problem solving. The group is challenged to complete tasks while working cooperatively.

ACTIVITY OBJECTIVES

1. Students will be able to efficiently practice the social skill of sharing.
2. Students will be able to identify their individual roles in the success of the group.
3. Students will be able to differentiate the value between individual achievements and the achievements of individuals working toward a common goal.

GRADE LEVELS   K-3

NHES STANDARDS   4, 5, 6

NASPE STANDARDS   2, 5

SUGGESTED TIME REQUIREMENTS   10 minutes

MATERIALS NEEDED

Lightweight balls such as beach balls, or foam balls to connect the "snake" (the larger the ball, the easier it is to connect the snake); an assortment of any of the following items spread around the room: beanbags, small pylons, balls of yarn, circus scarves, and any other items that won't roll away (each snake should be able to retrieve at least a dozen items, so you will need a dozen for each group); one wastebasket or hula hoop per group

PROCEDURE

1. Make an open space in the classroom for students to move around in. Arrange children in groups of four or five (snakes). Distribute the "food" around the classroom.

2. Have the snakes retreat to a corner of the room; this is their "den." Place a wastebasket or hula hoop in that area, which is where they will deposit all retrieved items.

3. Have students place the ball between their backs and the belly of the person behind them (for four children, there will be four balls; the first person or leader is required to hold a ball to his or her waist). The balls are not allowed to drop to the floor. The leader is not allowed to pick up food; the other members of the group should pick up the food.

4. It is the job of the front person to lead the snake around the room so they can collect as many pieces of food as possible.

5. The collected food is deposited into the snake's den.

6. The group must decide when to return to the den to deposit their food collection.

7. If the snake drops any of the balls that connect the students, they must return all the food they are carrying to you; redisperse the food around the room.

8. If the children are having difficulties, encourage them to switch positions and to strategize how they will be able to get to the food without dropping the balls.

9. Children should be reminded that the goal is to move together as a group and fill the snake's den with food without dropping the ball. Continue as time allows. Winning or losing is not the focus of the game; cooperation and strategy are.

SAFETY CONSIDERATIONS

Make sure the play area is free from desks and chairs. Use non-ball-type items as food so that they stay stationary. The size of the balls between children depends on their abilities; choose a ball that is light and allows for comfortable personal space between students.

TIPS AND VARIATIONS

When the children get the hang of it, tell them to switch positions by making a circle in their snake formation, reposition the balls, and have a new leader hold a ball to his or her waist and lead. Instead of using balls between students, you can use pool noodles that are placed under the arms of the group, freeing their hands to pick up food. The leader in this case is allowed to hold the noodles as they are placed under his or her arms.

BEAT THE CLOCK

AIM

This activity promotes the concepts of sharing, communication, and working toward a common goal. The group is challenged to complete a task while working cooperatively. In this activity, each team fills a wastebasket with balls as fast as they can. You are the timer and record which team does this the fastest. Because each member of the team must touch the ball, each team discusses and develops a strategy and defines and delineates roles for everyone in the group.

ACTIVITY OBJECTIVES

1. Students will be able to develop a strategy for this activity.
2. Students will be able to define a role for each member of the group.
3. Students will be able to cooperatively complete the task.
4. Students will be able to process their success or failure at the completion of this activity.

GRADE LEVELS   3-6

NHES STANDARDS   1, 4, 5, 6

NASPE STANDARDS   1, 2, 3, 5, 6

SUGGESTED TIME REQUIREMENTS   10 minutes

MATERIALS NEEDED

About 50 to 60 balls (tennis balls, balls of yarn, golf balls, or handballs); one large hula hoop or a chalk circle and chalk; one wastebasket or bin; stopwatch

PROCEDURE

1. Break students into groups of seven or eight. Tell students that they have to strategize a plan for completing this activity. The rules of the activity must be followed perfectly or the team is disqualified.

2. Inside a hula hoop or large chalk circle about three feet in diameter, place a wastebasket or bin full of some type of balls, at least 50 to 60 to make it fun.

3. Have two students from one group stand inside this hoop/chalk circle (for example, if you have a class of 24 students, there would be three different groups, with only one group participating at a time; each group puts two of its members inside the hoop when it is their

time to play). These two students cannot move from the circle or move their feet.

4. The other members of the group stand outside the hoop in some formation of their choosing.

5. Empty the container of all the balls and distribute them around the room. Dump the balls out of the basket from waist height to begin the round.

6. The object is to have each member of the group touch the ball before it is placed back into the basket.

7. The team members outside of the circle have two roles: two or three members are allowed to move anywhere in the play area to retrieve the balls, and the other two or three members must maintain a stationary position around the circle/hoop.

8. As each ball is retrieved, it must be passed around to every member of the group before it can be placed in the basket.

9. This can be frustrating if members of the group cannot catch well, but this can be alleviated if the group strategizes well (for example, students can pass or hand off the ball instead of throwing it, or they can roll the ball to each other). Students can be inventive when playing this game; some have made a chain or a second ring around the center ring; some have given numbers to all the group members so they do not forget anyone.

10. A ball that has not been touched by every member is put back into play.

11. The strategies will vary, and this should be encouraged because one strategy may not work for all groups. Before starting, give each group about two minutes to strategize. You are the official timekeeper and referee. This can be a timed event or play can continue until all the balls are placed in the wastebasket.

SAFETY CONSIDERATIONS
Make sure the play area is clear. Because only one group goes at a time, you may want the remaining students to form a circle around the participating team by sitting cross-legged. It can be their job to keep the balls in play, making sure they do not go under desks or radiators.

TIPS AND VARIATIONS
Students who have mobility limitations can take the center position or be the timekeeper, assistant referee, or strategy coach. This activity can be further processed by discussing how the team decided to proceed, who was in what position, what strategy was used, and what the team could have done better. The emphasis is on teamwork and equal participation.

INSIDE OUT

AIM

This activity is designed to increase health-enhancing levels of fitness, as well as increase the opportunity for cooperative play and provide participants with the opportunity to demonstrate responsible behaviors while having fun in a small setting.

ACTIVITY OBJECTIVES

1. Students will be able to work as a team to accomplish predetermined tasks as quickly as they can.
2. Students will be able to demonstrate their ability to use interpersonal communication skills to enhance the likelihood of success during this activity.
3. Students will be able to have the opportunity to engage in regular physical activity.

GRADE LEVELS K-6

NHES STANDARDS 1, 4, 5, 6

NASPE STANDARDS 1, 2, 3, 4, 5, 6

SUGGESTED TIME REQUIREMENTS 5-10 minutes

MATERIALS NEEDED

Several items are needed, such as books, bowling pins, balled-up paper, beanbags, balls, or erasers (one or two of each of the items are necessary; about 15 would be suitable); two hula hoops

PROCEDURE

1. In the center of the activity area, place one hula hoop and fill it with all of the items (approximately 15). Have about half of the students make a tight standing circle facing the center.

2. Have the remaining students form a circle around the first group, facing outward. Place the second hoop on the floor outside the second circle.

3. Pick one player from the first circle and one from the second circle to denote the start and the finish.

4. The object of the game is to move all the items from the center hoop to the outside hoop, touching every student in the room in the

process. The item is passed to each person in the inside circle; once it gets back to the start person, he or she passes it to the outside circle.

5. The students in the outside circle pass the item all around until it reaches the end person.

6. If anyone in any circle drops the object, it must be returned to the center hoop. If successful, the item is put into the outside hoop.

7. This activity continues until all the items are passed from the inside out.

8. This can be a timed event or it can be done at the pace set by the participants. For example, how many items can the group pass around in four minutes, or how long does it take to pass all the items around?

9. In the beginning, you can blow a whistle or clap your hands to let the starter know when to pass the next item. You can help pace this activity with quicker or slower starts so that it is challenging yet students still achieve success.

10. As they get the hang of it, they will develop a rhythm and strategy to pass the items without dropping them.

11. Keep track of the number of items and the time it took for the group to complete the task. Debrief by discussing strategy, cooperation, speed versus accuracy, shared responsibility, and so on.

SAFETY CONSIDERATIONS

Make sure the items are not too heavy.

TIPS AND VARIATIONS

The items can vary; using innovative equipment always adds to the excitement (rubber chickens, koosh balls, foam balls, clothespins, small action figures, and so on). Older children can pass around small weighted balls to make the activity more physically demanding.

4

Cooperative Games

Cooperative games are all about the joy, fun, and spirit of playing together. There is nothing nicer to witness than a group of children actually playing together and enjoying it, leaving no one out and not hurting one another. The games in this chapter have been used with children and adults alike. The promise of these activities is that every participant walks away feeling refreshed, joyful, and positive about themselves and others around them, all while learning a little something too. These cooperative games get children moving and playing; the educational aspects are discussed but do not necessarily have to be discussed with the participants. These games promote the values that we want for our children without having to hit them over the head with the message. Cooperation, a life skill often overlooked, is a key element in getting along with others; it is often not stressed until it becomes apparent that it is achingly absent.

UNTANGLE

AIM

This activity gets students to cooperate on several levels, to get a task completed, to communicate with one another, to have fun, and to realize that successful completion of these tasks is no accident.

ACTIVITY OBJECTIVES

1. Students will be able to untangle the ropes without letting go.
2. Students will be able to use their communication skills while participating in this activity.
3. All students will be able to participate and make a contribution to the group.
4. All students will be able to experience a positive interaction with their peers.

GRADE LEVELS K-6

NHES STANDARDS 1, 4, 5, 6

NASPE STANDARDS 1, 2, 3, 5, 6

SUGGESTED TIME REQUIREMENTS 10 minutes

MATERIALS NEEDED

One three-foot (1 m) piece of cotton rope knotted at both ends for each participant

PROCEDURE

1. Arrange the students into groups of five or six and have them make a small circle.

2. In the center of each group, place as many rope sections as there are participants.

3. Allow one student to arrange the ropes in a starburst fashion, criss-crossing all the ropes so that the ends are facing opposite sides of the circle.

4. Tell students to crouch down and grab hold of one knotted rope in each hand; they are not allowed to let go of the ropes or exchange hands.

5. When everyone has done this, tell them to slowly stand up, careful not to tug the ropes. All of the ropes will be tangled.

6. Tell the students to untangle the ropes and try to form a circle, never letting go of the ropes or switching hands to do so. Some students may be facing toward the circle and others may be facing out. Sometimes the group gets broken up into two smaller groups depending on how the untangling goes. Some may accomplish this quickly; others may take a while.

7. If the groups get frustrated, suggest a strategy; perhaps one member of the group could be the leader and give directions.

8. This activity can be repeated a few times; you can change participants or make groups larger or smaller to support challenge or success.

SAFETY CONSIDERATIONS

Students should be told to never put the ropes around their necks or anyone else's. Tell them not to swing or whip the ropes around. Using cotton clothesline is best because it is more forgiving. Keep the length of the rope to no more than three feet (a little less than 1 m).

TIPS AND VARIATIONS

You may also have the students do this with no spoken words at first, then repeat with communication. The differences will be stark. Adding more students per group provides increased challenge. You may also challenge students to do this against the clock or each other.

CRUNCH TIME

AIM

This activity involves as many students as possible in passing items to one another using their feet and legs only. Use various objects found wherever you are; for example, if you are in the classroom, you can use a board eraser, book, empty can, or pencil box. This activity calls into action cooperative teamwork, interpersonal communication skills, decision making, and goal setting. It also challenges personal fitness levels (abdominal strength).

ACTIVITY OBJECTIVES

1. Students will be able to pass items to one another without the use of their hands.
2. Students will be able to cooperate with one another.
3. Students will be able to identify that cooperation is the key to achieving the task.
4. Students will be able to identify the value in allowing everyone to participate.

GRADE LEVELS K-6

NHES STANDARDS   1, 2, 4, 6

NASPE STANDARDS   1, 2, 3, 4, 5, 6

SUGGESTED TIME REQUIREMENTS   10 minutes

MATERIALS NEEDED

One hula hoop per group; about six of the following: balls, cones, erasers, plastic cups, water bottles, sheets of paper, rope segments, board erasers, and so on per group

PROCEDURE

1. Have students sit on the floor, one behind the other, with their feet in front of them and their hands at their sides.

2. Place a hula hoop at the end of the line and several objects at the beginning of the line. This is the starting point.

3. The person at the front picks up one object with his or her feet (only) and passes it to the person behind him or her.

4. This can be done by passing the object over the head or by swinging the legs to the side to pass the object to the student who is next in line.

5. If passing over the head, alert children to pay attention to the person in front.

6. Students can use their hands for balance only. They cannot use their hands to pick up the object. This sounds easy, but after a few turns participants will tire because they are using their often-neglected abdominal muscles. The object is for everyone to achieve the task of passing the objects to the end of the line where the last person places the objects into the hoop. If they had fun, they've won!

7. You can pace this activity as you see fit, either allowing the first person to pass the next object immediately or have the group wait until the previous object is passed all the way to the end.

SAFETY CONSIDERATIONS

Many students will find it somewhat difficult to use their legs and feet. They will have less control and may kick each other, so you may want to have them take their shoes off. If you have limited space, make the groups smaller and have them sit in circles.

TIPS AND VARIATIONS

You might want to change the arrangement, perhaps having students sit in a circle facing the middle. Denote a starting and ending point and tell the students that the end person is the one who places the object in the hoop in the center of the group's circle. You can also have a circle-within-a-circle configuration. Have the beginning person from the inner circle retrieve the object from the center hoop and have the students pass it around to all the participants in the inner circle. When this is completed, the last person in the inner circle passes it to a student in the outer circle; the object is passed around to all. This continues until all the objects have passed through the entire group. Objects can be placed in another hoop outside the outer circle. You can use a timer and see if they can set a group record. This activity is similar to the Inside Out activity in chapter 3, but children use their feet instead.

ALL TOGETHER NOW

AIM

This activity engages the mind, body, and spirit in a truly cooperative way. This activity is more difficult than some of the others in this book, but yields a larger reward when accomplished.

ACTIVITY OBJECTIVES

1. Students will be able to work in small groups to pass around a rope.
2. Students will be able to cooperate with one another so that every person in the group experiences success.
3. Students will be able to identify that cooperation is the key to achieving the task.
4. Students will be able to identify the value in allowing everyone to participate.

GRADE LEVELS   4-6

NHES STANDARDS   4, 5, 6

NASPE STANDARDS   1, 2, 3, 5, 6

SUGGESTED TIME REQUIREMENTS   10 minutes

MATERIALS NEEDED

At minimum, two sets of ropes will be needed for this activity. Cotton clothesline is recommended because of its soft texture and because it is relatively inexpensive. Using a rope with an approximate length of 20 feet (6 m), tie a knot in the center of the rope. Then tie both ends together, forming a rope circle that has a diameter of approximately 6 feet (2 m). You may have to adjust the length of the rope to best suit your space. You can use several ropes of this size to accommodate your group, provided you have the space to allow more than one group to play at a time. You can also create a larger rope circle with a longer length of rope to accommodate more participants; a 30-foot rope (about 9 m) will allow a few more students to participate.

PROCEDURE

1. Arrange students into groups of five or six.

2. Have one group demonstrate first, using a smaller circle of rope. Tell each student to grab a part of the rope with both hands and face each other in a circle.

3. At first, have the students leave some slack in the rope.

4. At the count of three, the rope is passed through the hands of each person in the group, each touching the knot as it goes around.

5. The second time, ask students to make the rope taut by leaning back while holding onto the rope with two hands.

6. The tension in the rope will be obvious; the task now is to pass the rope around the group so that everyone touches the knot and no one falls over.

7. Once this is accomplished, add other activities, such as having the group sit down as a unit, get up as a unit, or lift one leg and sit, all while the rope is taut.

8. This is a challenging activity. Once some success has been met, bring out the larger rope and add additional participants. The rope can be big enough to accommodate the entire class.

9. You can repeat the movements as done with the smaller group.

SAFETY CONSIDERATIONS

Check the knotted end of the ropes each time you do this activity. Make sure the play area is free from anything students can get hurt on; someone will fall. Demonstrate the proper speed to pass the rope around so no one gets rope burn.

TIPS AND VARIATIONS

Adding more or fewer students to the mix is always fun. You can also vary the activity by changing the movements the group must perform as they maintain their grip on the rope. You can add a speed challenge or tasks that involve any combination of movements.

ALPHABET RELAY

AIM

This activity is a real crowd-pleaser because it allows and promotes the varied strengths of all participants. The activity uses physical strength, physical fitness, coordination, literacy skills, decision making, leadership, and cooperation.

ACTIVITY OBJECTIVES

1. Students will be able to create health and wellness words using alphabet letters.
2. Students will be able to exert their unique qualities in concert to help the group succeed.
3. Students will be able to demonstrate that cooperation between group members is a key element for the group's success and enjoyment.

GRADE LEVELS   1-6

NHES STANDARDS   1, 4, 5, 6, 7, 8

NASPE STANDARDS   1, 2, 3, 5, 6

SUGGESTED TIME REQUIREMENTS   10 minutes

MATERIALS NEEDED

For a group of 30 participants you will need several sets of alphabet letters, either the refrigerator type or laminated cutouts (approximately 10 sets); four cones or pylons; one hula hoop

PROCEDURE

1. Break the group into four even teams.

2. Clear out the play area and place the four cones so they create a large square.

3. Have each team sit behind their cone, facing the center.

4. Place all of the alphabet pieces in a hula hoop in the center of the square.

5. Tell the students that they will crab-walk from their cone into the center of the square and retrieve one alphabet piece per trip. Students can place the alphabet piece on their abdomens as they crab-walk out of the center and place the piece behind the cone when they return.

6. Allow only one member of the team to crab-walk at a time. Because crab-walking can be very difficult for some and tiring for all, allow participants to alternate fetching letters and spelling and creating words and phrases. Allowing individuals to choose and exert their individual strengths in this activity provides a huge sense of autonomy—some may fetch letters, another may be the speller, and another may be calling out what letters to retrieve.

7. The object is to retrieve as many alphabet pieces as possible and use these pieces to create words or a phrase in answer to your request. The question or request is announced at the start of the activity; possible requests include creating a list of healthy snacks, listing exercises that maintain fitness, listing all the green fruits and vegetables the students know of, or filling in the blanks; for example, _____ and _____ are examples of risk factors associated with heart disease/cancer/stroke. The questions are endless.

SAFETY CONSIDERATIONS
Keeping the alphabet letters within a hoop or bucket will keep the letters from flying around. Younger or less fit children will become very tired from this activity.

TIPS AND VARIATIONS
If there are students who are impaired in any way, they can provide leadership or literacy skills from wherever they are (such as a wheelchair or seat). You could also have students create their own questions or requests; these can be randomly drawn as the play begins.

BUILD A BETTER LETTER

AIM

This activity gets participants to use their minds and bodies in a novel way and to cooperate with one another and have fun doing so.

ACTIVITY OBJECTIVES

1. Students will be able to cooperate with their peers to create letters, numbers, or shapes with their bodies in response to your questions.

2. Students will use group decision-making processes to answer questions.

3. Students will be able to use their unique and collective coordination skills.

4. Students will be able to use leadership skills.

GRADE LEVELS   K-6

NHES STANDARDS   1, 2, 4, 5, 6, 7

NASPE STANDARDS   1, 2, 3, 5, 6

SUGGESTED TIME REQUIREMENTS   10 minutes

MATERIALS NEEDED

None

PROCEDURE

1. Have the students break up into groups of five or six.

2. When this is done, assign each group an area within the play space. You can prepare some health- and wellness-oriented questions before the activity begins.

3. Students are required to answer the question using their bodies to depict a letter, shape, or number. Here are some possible questions: How many hours of sleep should students your age get each night? (This requires the students to make the number 10.) Which fruit has the most vitamin C? (This requires the students to make the shape of an orange or lemon.) Which of the following activities is best suited for maintaining cardiorespiratory fitness? (The students could form an A for weight training, B for cycling, or C for video gaming.) The groups should choose the best answer together and form that letter, number, or shape as a group.

SAFETY CONSIDERATIONS

Keep the play area clear and caution children to watch out for each other and not to step on each other's fingers and hands. You may allow students to remove their shoes for this activity.

TIPS AND VARIATIONS

Keep the questions age appropriate for maximum enjoyment. If there are students who are impaired in any way, they can provide leadership or direction from wherever they are (such as a wheelchair or seat). You can have all the teams work together to form a word, number, or shape. If the groups are spelling a word, each group would be responsible for a single letter.

SPARE SQUARE TEAM TAG

AIM
This activity gets everyone involved in a cooperative effort to share circus squares or silks for points.

ACTIVITY OBJECTIVES
1. Students will be able to move around the play area in self-space.
2. Students will be able to help their team win points by sharing their spare square.
3. Students will be able to identify that cooperation is a key element in the team's success.

GRADE LEVELS   K-6

NHES STANDARDS   4

NASPE STANDARDS   1, 2, 3, 4, 5, 6

SUGGESTED TIME REQUIREMENTS   10 minutes

MATERIALS NEEDED
Different-colored circus squares or circus silks (bandannas or fabric squares can also be used, or different-colored pinnies), one for each participant

PROCEDURE
1. Break up the group into two teams.

2. You might want to distribute like-colored circus squares, or bandannas or fabric squares to differentiate the teams.

3. Each player is given a square or bandanna to place in a back pocket or waistband.

4. The object of the game is to have all the players move in self-space without bumping into one another.

5. As students move around the play area, they will be trying to steal the squares from the opposing team's pockets or waistbands.

6. If a square is stolen, that player must freeze in that spot; he or she can only be freed by a team member who goes under the frozen player's legs and hands over his or her own square to the teammate.

7. At that point, the player without a square remains frozen until another teammate frees him or her by crawling between the legs and sharing the square.

8. Every time a player shares his or her square, a point is awarded to the team. There are two basic rules: Squares must always be visible at all times, hanging from the pocket or waistband, and squares cannot be stolen while one player is freeing another.

9. At first the students may be reluctant to free their teammates because it will cause them to be frozen. However, remind them that they win by sharing their spare square and cooperating—sharing equals points. The game concludes when one team is completely frozen or the allotted time runs out. Even though an entire team may be frozen, they could win because they have the most shared squares.

SAFETY CONSIDERATIONS
Clear the play area so there is nothing to bump into or step on.

TIPS AND VARIATIONS
You can change the rules a little and tell students that once each individual student has shared a square three times, he or she can sit in a line or in some other formation (for example, make a circle or a letter with his or her body). The team that completes this task first wins. Depending on the size of the play area, you may choose to have the players slow or quicken the pace as you deem appropriate.

PARACHUTE POPCORN BLAST

AIM
This activity requires the entire class to work together to get popcorn balls into a wastebasket with a parachute, which takes a lot of cooperation and some patience.

ACTIVITY OBJECTIVES
1. Students will be able to blast the popcorn from the parachute into the waiting wastebaskets.
2. Students will be able to demonstrate communication and cooperative skills to accomplish this task.

GRADE LEVELS   3-6

NHES STANDARDS   1, 4, 5, 6

NASPE STANDARDS   1, 2, 3, 4, 5, 6

SUGGESTED TIME REQUIREMENTS   10 minutes

MATERIALS NEEDED
One parachute or large bedsheet; several popcorn balls (Wiffle balls, balls of yarn, koosh balls, foam balls, or slightly deflated rubber playground balls can also be used); two or three wastebaskets

PROCEDURE
1. Clear the play area and tell all of the students to grab the parachute/sheet with both hands.

2. Set up the wastebaskets on chairs or desks behind the players.

3. Demonstrate how to move the parachute by rippling and waving it; the students will catch on quickly.

4. Briefly discuss the objective of the game as well as the cooperative skills necessary for success.

5. Challenge students to try to pop a ball from the parachute towards a wastebasket and attempt to get a ball (sink) in the basket.

6. Have students predict the number of baskets they will sink (balls they will get into the wastebasket) and let them go.

7. Begin by using just one ball in the parachute at a time so that they can work on their cooperative efforts. They will soon see what it will take to succeed. You can add another ball or two to make it more interesting as the students start to understand the activity.

SAFETY CONSIDERATIONS

If you are in a classroom, be mindful of overhead lights or fixtures and use an appropriate ball for indoor play.

TIPS AND VARIATIONS

Vary the size and type of ball to ensure success or add challenge to the activity. Younger children can also enjoy this with balloons or beach balls.

Inclusion Games

This chapter looks at inclusion in two ways: It presents activities that can be engaged by typical students so that they realize that others may have different skill or ability levels, and it presents activities that can be enjoyed by all students. Children are all the same in their desire to have fun and be involved despite the level of their abilities. These activities are offered to teachers, counselors, group leaders, and students to meet the challenges of inclusion. They may help facilitate a change in culture by creating a more positive and accepting environment. These classroom-tested activities can be modified for students of any ability or skill level.

EXPLAIN IT TO ME (PART 1)

AIM
This activity allows students to practice communication skills with their peers in a nonthreatening way. It also provides an opportunity for students to learn about the various ways individuals articulate messages and process information and how this influences behavior.

ACTIVITY OBJECTIVES
1. Students will be able to organize their thoughts and communicate instructions to their peers.
2. Students will be able to practice public-speaking skills.
3. Students will be able to recognize the differences and similarities in speaking and listening abilities.

GRADE LEVELS   3-6

NHES STANDARDS   2, 4, 8

NASPE STANDARDS   5

SUGGESTED TIME REQUIREMENTS   5-10 minutes

MATERIALS NEEDED
12 index cards, a marker, and a pencil and paper for all participants

PROCEDURE
1. Draw several shapes on index cards. These shapes can overlap or be within one another or next to one another (see figures, pages 67-70). The shapes can be more or less complicated as you deem appropriate. It is best to have several of the index cards prepared ahead of time.

2. Have a student volunteer to select a card. Tell him or her to hold the card so that no one can see the shape.

3. Tell the students that the volunteer will attempt to give clear instructions so that they might be able to replicate the shape on their own papers. The only rule is that the volunteer can use words only and listeners are not allowed to ask any questions.

4. When the volunteer is done giving directions, have him or her show the others the shape.

5. Ask students to hold up their individual drawings and compare.

6. There will be some variations in the drawings; ask students why this was so difficult, and ask the volunteer if this was easy or difficult and why.

7. Allow other volunteers to give the directions; when done, cite apparent changes in communication styles or skills. Some students may become frustrated with this activity, so be mindful of the difficulty of the shapes.

▶ Sample shapes.

(continued)

(continued)

▶ Sample shapes.

SAFETY CONSIDERATIONS

None.

TIPS AND VARIATIONS

You may want to allow students to ask questions for clarification purposes. You may want to highlight differences in communication

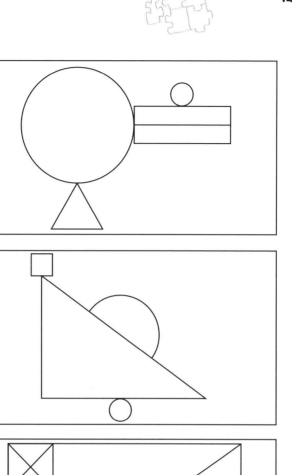

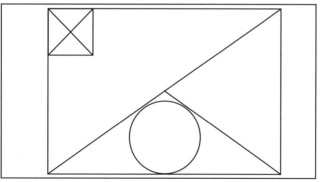

▶ Sample shapes.

(continued)

styles and abilities or the possible effects of language barriers, dialect, or hearing impairments. You may want to discuss different styles of learning; for example, how some children learn best when they listen, others when they can read directions, and others when they can actively perform or do things.

(continued)

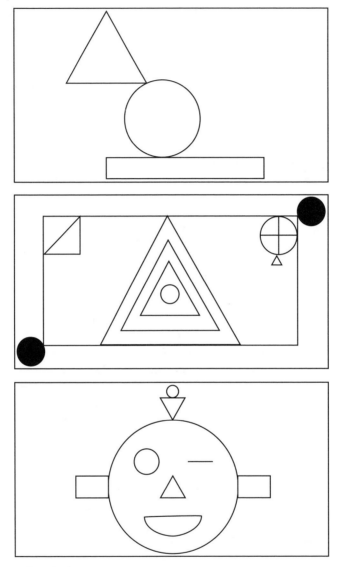

▶ Sample shapes.

EXPLAIN IT TO ME (PART 2)

AIM

This activity allows students to practice communication skills among their peers in a nonthreatening way. It also provides an opportunity for students to learn about the different ways individuals articulate messages and process information and how this influences behavior. This activity also allows students to physically interact with one another in a cooperative and noncompetitive way.

ACTIVITY OBJECTIVES

1. Students will be able to organize their thoughts and communicate instructions to their peers.
2. Students will be able to practice public-speaking skills.
3. Students will be able to recognize the differences and similarities in speaking and listening abilities.
4. Students will be able to work in small groups and practice communication and decision-making skills.

GRADE LEVELS   5-6

NHES STANDARDS   2, 4, 5, 6, 7

NASPE STANDARDS   1, 2, 3, 4, 5, 6

SUGGESTED TIME REQUIREMENTS   10 minutes

MATERIALS NEEDED

12 index cards, a marker, and a pencil and paper for all participants

PROCEDURE

1. Draw simple, four- or five-line shapes on the index cards. These shapes can overlap or be within one another as long as the human body can replicate that shape without harm or discomfort. The shapes can be more or less complicated as you deem appropriate (see figure, page 72). Have several index cards prepared ahead of time.

2. Have students break up into groups of six or seven.

3. One person will choose a shape card and hold the card so that no one can see the shape.

4. Tell the students that the volunteer will attempt to give clear instructions so that they can replicate the shape on the floor with their own bodies.

5. Students with disabilities can be the reader or can participate to the best of their ability. The only rule is that the volunteer can use words only and listeners are not allowed to ask any questions.

6. When the volunteer is done giving directions, have him or her show the others the shape.

7. Ask the students why this was so difficult, and ask the volunteer if this was easy or difficult and why.

8. Allow other volunteers to give the directions; when done, cite apparent changes in communication styles or skills. Some students may become frustrated with this activity, so be mindful of the difficulty of the shapes.

▶ Sample shapes.

SAFETY CONSIDERATIONS

Make sure the play area is free from chairs and desks or anything else that students can get hurt on. Students with disabilities may need assistance in maneuvering wheelchairs, walkers, or crutches.

TIPS AND VARIATIONS

You may want to allow students to ask questions for clarification purposes. You may want to highlight differences in communication styles and abilities or the possible effects of language barriers, dialect, or hearing and physical limitations.

Talk about different styles of learning and how some children learn best when they listen, others when they can read, and others when they actively do things. Depending on the grade level, you might introduce the terms *language comprehension, auditory processing,* or *visual learning.*

BEACH BALL CONVERSATION

AIM

This activity is aimed at improving communication skills for all participants by providing the opportunity to share thoughts, feelings, and experiences using a low-key and informal approach.

ACTIVITY OBJECTIVES

1. Students will be able to share thoughts, feelings, and experiences with their classmates.

2. Students will be able to demonstrate that communicating with one another can enhance their personal health.

3. Students will be able to recognize that we all experience life around us differently.

GRADE LEVELS   K-6

NHES STANDARDS   1, 2, 4, 7

NASPE STANDARDS   1, 2, 5, 6

SUGGESTED TIME REQUIREMENTS   5-10 minutes

MATERIALS NEEDED

Large beach ball or large balloon; one marker

PROCEDURE

1. This activity allows students to play where they are, either from their chairs or the floor. There is no reason to move desks, chairs, or equipment as long as students can throw and catch a beach ball or large balloon where they are seated or stationed.

2. You can inflate the beach ball or balloon beforehand; deciding which to use depends on the ability of your least-skilled participant. A large beach ball that is not fully inflated is easily handled and slow-moving. A large inflated balloon is slower still, but for obvious reasons is less forgiving. Assess your group and choose a ball or balloon accordingly.

3. Most beach balls are separated by sections, often differentiated by color; taking advantage of this design, you can write simple talking points on each section (see figure, page 75). If using the balloon, you can write these talking points in circles or section the balloon similar to the vertical sections on a hot air balloon.

Suggested talking points for Beach Ball Conversation.

4. The talking points can be about anything; here are some examples: I am most happy when . . .; What I like most about my life is . . .; I am interested in . . .; In my spare time I like to . . .; My favorite game is . . .; I am good at . . .; What I want most of all is . . .; I am . . .; I believe . . .; I am different because . . .; I worry about . . .; I wonder . . .; I hear . . .; I want . . .; I pretend . . .; I understand . . .; I dream . . .; I say . . .; I try . . .; I cry . . .

5. For the kindergarten through 1st-grade crowd, you may want to use drawings of faces depicting happiness, sadness, surprise, anger, worry, laughter, crying, and so on. This will alleviate anxiety regarding reading ability with younger participants.

6. From where they are in the room, students toss, hit, or pass the ball or balloon around the room.

7. When someone catches it, he or she looks at the closest panel and reacts to the question or prompt. This answer can be simple or you may ask them to expand on the answer depending on the time allotted for the activity.

8. If the same person gets the ball or balloon twice, he or she passes it to the nearest person so that he or she gets a turn.

9. If students need to warm up to the exercise, allow them the option to "pass" once. However, the next time they receive the ball they must participate.

SAFETY CONSIDERATIONS

This is a slow-moving activity that can be done seated in chairs or in a circle; however, remind students that they should not lunge or grab at the ball or balloon because everyone will get a chance. Have a second balloon prepared in the event of a breakage.

TIPS AND VARIATIONS

You can make this more interesting by using music and playing it like hot potato. You may also want to encourage students to ask other students questions in an effort to get to know them better. For example, if a student catches the ball, he or she answers the question on the ball or balloon; you may then allow another student to ask a secondary question to prompt more communication.

MAP QUEST

AIM

This activity allows students to practice communication skills among their peers in a fun and novel way. It also provides an opportunity for students to learn about the different ways individuals articulate messages and process information and how this influences behavior.

ACTIVITY OBJECTIVES

1. Students will be able to organize their thoughts and communicate instructions to their peers.
2. Students will be able to communicate to one another in a way that is clear and articulate.
3. Students will be able to complete a task as a result of following verbal directions as given by their partner.
4. Students will be able to recognize the differences and similarities in speaking and listening abilities.

GRADE LEVELS 4-6

NHES STANDARDS 2, 4, 5, 6

NASPE STANDARDS 1, 2, 5, 6

SUGGESTED TIME REQUIREMENTS 15 minutes

MATERIALS NEEDED

Blindfolds for half the students in the class (bandannas or sweatbands work also); index cards with maps and directional cues written on one side and tasks on the other (about 12 prepared index cards; students will use the map to get to the task stations to complete the task); pylons or cones, poly spots, jump ropes, beanbags, baskets, buckets, hula hoops, and other equipment (used to perform the tasks written on the directional cards)

PROCEDURE

1. This activity takes a little preparation before introducing it to the class. First you must set up a number of task stations (see figures on pages 78 and 79 for sample maps and stations). These stations will be equipped with the objects necessary for completing an activity that will be performed by the blindfolded participant. Students are paired two to a team.

2. Individual activities must be written on an index card in their briefest form. Here is an example: You must place three beanbags under the bucket after you have skipped rope three times while standing inside a hula hoop.

3. The activities can be relatively easy; the catch is that the blindfolded participant must first find the task station. This is done by listening to the map directions as read by the other partner. Map directions are written on the other side of the index card.

4. Maps and directional cues should be given simply. Here's an example: Starting at cone 1, take six steps forward, turn right, take two big steps to the left and one step over the obstacle (two cones with a ruler on top), get down on all fours, and crawl under the hurdle.

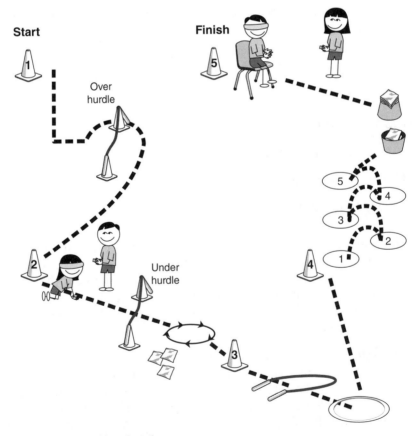

▶ Sample map with task stations.

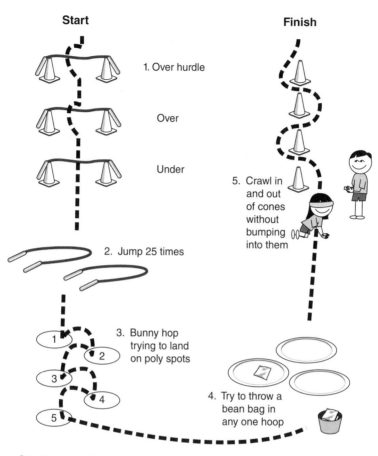

▶ Sample map with task stations *(continued)*.

5. After one member of the pair has gotten to the task station via the map and completed the task according to the directions on the card, the students switch roles and start from the beginning with a new card.

6. Map directions and task assignments should be put on the same card. These can be used over again so there is no need to re-create maps and tasks; thus, the materials remain constant each time you want to use this activity.

SAFETY CONSIDERATIONS

There is always a chance that students will bump into one another or any chairs and desks in their way. Clear out the activity area as best you can.

TIPS AND VARIATIONS

Keep directions simple at first; if students are successful, you can have more difficult map quests and more challenging tasks. Another alternative is to set up a mini-obstacle course in the play area or outside using cones, hoops, and poly spots. The non-blindfolded student can give verbal directions to the blindfolded partner so he or she can make it through the obstacle course safely and successfully. This can be done as a race against the clock or, if two identical courses are created, students can race against another set of participants.

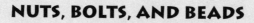

NUTS, BOLTS, AND BEADS

AIM
This activity illustrates the frustration faced by some children with compromised or latent motor skill development.

ACTIVITY OBJECTIVES
1. Students will be able to identify some of the difficulties experienced by others with motor difficulties.
2. Students will be able to experience firsthand some level of difficulty as they participate in this activity.

GRADE LEVELS   2-6

NHES STANDARDS   8

NASPE STANDARDS   2, 5, 6

SUGGESTED TIME REQUIREMENTS   10 minutes

MATERIALS NEEDED
A pair of large canvas garden gloves; a large bolt and nut; a length of string (knotted on one side); 10 medium-sized wooden beads; and a plastic jar with a screw-top lid (plastic mayonnaise jars work well) for each group

PROCEDURE
1. Depending on the number of sets you have created, break students into groups of three or four.

2. Each group gets a pair of gloves and a jar containing a nut and bolt set, 10 wooden beads, and a length of string.

3. Students can sit on the floor or at their desks; the goal is for everyone in the group to complete the following tasks:

    a. one student puts on the oversized gloves

    b. opens the jar

    c. takes the nut and fastens it completely to the bolt and then does it in reverse

    d. places the nut and bolt back in the jar

    e. threads the 10 beads onto the string

    f. removes the beads and puts them back in the jar along with the string

g. fastens the top of the jar

h. removes the gloves

i. passes the gloves and the jar to the next person

4. This can be done as a relay; you can challenge groups to have each member complete the task, and the first group to finish wins.

SAFETY CONSIDERATIONS

Make the beads large enough to be handled with the gloves and large enough to collect easily when they are dropped on the floor. Square wooden beads are a good option because they don't roll as easily, and they don't look like something a student might want to eat!

TIPS AND VARIATIONS

If students are frustrated, make that the teachable moment. To diminish some frustration, use larger nuts, bolts, and beads. If this is still difficult, have students wear just one glove. You may want to use a wing nut instead of a traditional hex nut. You can also introduce the task of threading a piece of yarn through holes in some cardboard.

(NOT) SEEING IS BELIEVING!

AIM

This activity demonstrates the difficulties that some people experience because of visual impairments or limitations.

ACTIVITY OBJECTIVES

1. Students will be able to identify some of the difficulties experienced by a person whose vision is impaired because they will experience some level of difficulty as they participate in this activity.

2. Students will be able to experience firsthand a similar level of difficulty as they participate in this activity.

GRADE LEVELS   2-6

NHES STANDARDS   8

NASPE STANDARDS   2, 5, 6

SUGGESTED TIME REQUIREMENTS   15 minutes

MATERIALS NEEDED

One pair of plastic safety goggles for every two students (scratch the lenses entirely to obstruct the view); several pylons or cones, hula hoops, balloons, beach balls, kickballs, and beanbags; prepared action cards to accompany each station (this card explains what is to be done at the station; the non-goggled student gives verbal directions)

PROCEDURE

1. Set up the obstacle course. Place stations around the perimeter of the room, giving enough room between each station to accommodate two people and the passing of groups. At each station, the goggled participant will have to complete simple tasks with minimal guidance from his or her assistant. The action cards can be taped to the pylon.

2. Pair students; one participant wears the goggles while the other assists him or her through the obstacle course. The assistant remains within an arm's length of their partner at all times.

3. The goggled student is not completely blinded and may have some vision with the goggles on. The assistant is there for support and guidance only as needed.

4. The tasks can be, for example, to walk through a small slalom course, bounce a balloon off specified body parts, throw and catch a beach ball with the nongoggled partner, toss a beanbag into a hula hoop that is placed on the floor, and get a kickball into the wastebasket. Each activity represents a separate station.

5. You can vary the activities to best match your available resources.

6. Have each pair try to complete the task in a given amount of time (for example, 30 to 40 seconds) and switch to the next station.

7. When everyone has tried each station, let the partners switch positions. At this time you may want to slightly change the tasks so as not to give an unfair advantage.

SAFETY CONSIDERATIONS

Make sure that the activity area is free and clear of any obstacles other than the ones you place in the game. The obstructed view of the goggles can disorient some participants; tell them to remove the goggles immediately if they feel dizzy.

TIPS AND VARIATIONS

If students are frustrated, make that the teachable moment. You might want to keep frustration at a minimum because you want everyone to work through the tasks and not quit before they get started. If you have many students and space is limited, reduce the number of tasks and stations. You can put three in a group and have students take turns trying to complete a task within their group in one place.

YOU SAID WHAT?

AIM

This activity demonstrates that people often have varied auditory skills; not everyone hears what is being said and not everyone always understands what is being said.

ACTIVITY OBJECTIVES

1. Students will be able to identify some of the difficulties experienced by a person whose hearing is impaired.
2. Students will be able to experience firsthand a similar level of difficulty as they participate in this activity.

GRADE LEVELS   K-6

NHES STANDARDS   8

NASPE STANDARDS   2, 5, 6

SUGGESTED TIME REQUIREMENTS   5-10 minutes

MATERIALS NEEDED

Enough cotton for placing in the ears of each student; poster board or chalkboard

PROCEDURE

1. Ahead of time, prepare a poster or put some pictures or stick drawings on the chalkboard of some task that you want the students to complete in self-space.

2. The visual directions should be vague; only give enough information so that students get a minimal understanding of what is expected of them. Essentially, you want them to have to hear the verbal instructions to get it right.

3. You can start out by saying, "Can everyone hear me all right?" When they reply in the affirmative, give them just a little more information, such as "Look at the directions on the board; please follow them and do what is asked."

4. You should instruct students to get started and then provide further information in a quiet voice or some made-up language.

5. If you speak softly, only those students nearest you will hear; if you speak in a made-up language, none of the participants will be really successful. You can decide.

6. The task can be very simple, such as stand, turn completely around, and then sit facing the window and put your hands on your head.

7. Students will soon see that they are getting only limited information or information that they can't decipher.

8. Tell the students who completed the task what a good job they did and tell the ones who didn't that you are disappointed.

9. When they complain, discuss issues like audio impairments, language barriers, and comprehension. They will hear your message loud and clear!

SAFETY CONSIDERATIONS

Depending on the task, keep the activity area free and clear of any obstacles. If you provided cotton for their ears, make sure you collect and dispose of all of it before children move on to the next class or go home.

TIPS AND VARIATIONS

You might want to give all directions in a made-up language only, or ask students to figure out the task by looking at the (incomplete) directions on the board. Only provide them with enough information to get them going. You may also want to distribute cotton to some students to plug their ears, then give some direction and watch them scramble.

WHAT WOULD YOU DO IF...

AIM

This activity is truly one in which all students can participate. The purpose is to allow students to react in any capacity they want or can. The main idea is to get students to sit or stand in self-space and allow them to react in an active way to the sentences read by you. There is no wrong way to play; the only limit is the students' imaginations.

ACTIVITY OBJECTIVES

1. Students will be able to act out each sentence to the best of their abilities for 30 seconds.
2. Students will be able to use their imagination to create sentences to add to the story line.
3. Students will be able to organize their thoughts and communicate instructions to their peers.
4. Students will be able to practice communicating to one another in a way that is clear and articulate.

GRADE LEVELS K-3

NHES STANDARDS 1, 4, 5, 7

NASPE STANDARDS 1, 2, 3, 4, 5, 6

SUGGESTED TIME REQUIREMENTS 5-10 minutes

MATERIALS NEEDED

Pre-scripted scenarios to facilitate the activity

PROCEDURE

1. This activity can be very informal depending on your creativity.

2. You can use pre-scripted sentences to facilitate the activity or you can be creative and develop scenarios based on previous lessons, activities, or discussions.

3. You can begin by saying, "Today we'll use our imaginations, and we'll pretend to take a walk or ride through the jungle. . . . What would you do if it started to rain?"

4. Help them get started by lifting and opening your imaginary umbrella.

5. From a seated or standing position, have students continuously walking or motioning (in place) as if they were walking through the jungle.

6. While walking (in place) and holding your umbrella, tell the students that a large swarm of flies are coming, and they must swat them to keep from getting bitten (have them swat flies for 30 seconds).

7. You can add health-promoting messages such as this: "Don't forget to apply sunscreen and use bug repellent."

8. After your story has taken off, you can ask students to add a sentence and have their classmates act out the action. Once students have done this activity, they will be eager and more prepared to contribute.

SAFETY CONSIDERATIONS

Students with disabilities can perform this activity wherever they are most comfortable; either standing or sitting (as if they were in a boat) works equally well. Make sure there is enough room between students so they do not hit each other with their movements.

TIPS AND VARIATIONS

This is a movement-oriented activity; however, it is important to emphasize that we all don't react the same way—individuality is the emphasis. This is a great activity for you to infuse concepts such as health promotion and reducing health risks, emphasize safe behaviors, and simulate health-enhancing behaviors.

KOPY KAT

AIM

This activity allows children of any ability to move as best they can in self-space. The object of the game is for one person in the group to lead the actions and movements of the group discreetly; another student who is brought to the group after the leader has started the movements must guess who is orchestrating the movements.

ACTIVITY OBJECTIVES

1. Students will be able to follow the nonverbal cues of their classmates and move to the best of their ability.
2. Students will be able to practice their leadership skills in an informal, low-key activity.

GRADE LEVELS K-3

NHES STANDARDS 2, 4

NASPE STANDARDS 1, 2, 3, 5, 6

SUGGESTED TIME REQUIREMENTS 5-10 minutes

MATERIALS NEEDED

None

PROCEDURE

1. Have students sit in a circle facing one another in the center of the play area. They can sit in chairs or on the floor.
2. One student (the onlooker) is sent out of the room or away from the play area with his or her back to the circle.
3. A leader is chosen, and he or she begins a repetitive gesture or motion that his or her colleagues can follow.
4. Bring the onlooker back to the circle once the initial movement has begun.
5. Changes in activity and multiple gestures by the leader should be done subtly so that the onlooker has difficulty figuring out who is leading the group.

6. Remind students that they should pay attention to the leader and follow changes in activity as they see it.

7. The onlooker gets two guesses to figure out the leader. This activity can continue as long as time is allowed. Swap out leaders and onlookers so that many students get an opportunity.

SAFETY CONSIDERATIONS

The abilities of any physically challenged students should dictate whether the class is on the floor or is seated.

TIPS AND VARIATIONS

Both physically challenged and typical students will like this activity because they can participate in their own capacity.

Energizing Activities

These activities invigorate your group. They are used as a way to increase movement opportunities throughout the day and can be done using limited space. These activities are great for recapturing that after-recess energy or to energize students when they get too comfortable, sleepy, or disengaged.

FRIDAY FREAK-OUT

AIM

This activity is a big favorite and is requested often, so much so that I started to use it on a daily basis. Despite the name, you can use this anytime to get your students revved up. The main idea is to get students up and moving in an informal, self-directed, expressive way.

ACTIVITY OBJECTIVES

1. Students will be able to move, dance, and express themselves in self-space in their own unique style.
2. Students will be able to enjoy this movement activity for the sake of fun.
3. Students will be able to demonstrate respect and responsible behavior toward others while participating.
4. Students will have the opportunity to engage in regular physical activity.

GRADE LEVELS   K-6

NHES STANDARDS   1, 7

NASPE STANDARDS   1, 3, 4, 5, 6

SUGGESTED TIME REQUIREMENTS   5-10 minutes

MATERIALS NEEDED

Radio, CD player, or MP3 player (preselect the music so that it is age appropriate and reflective of the musical genre appreciated by the intended audience); circus squares or silks, one for each participant

PROCEDURE

1. Briefly explain that students should move their bodies in any way they like.

2. They must keep their movements safe in that they do not bump or hit anyone in the process.

3. Students are to move (dance) until they hear the music stop.

4. When the music stops, they freeze; give them a few seconds to catch their breath and restore order before the next round. At this

time, you can ask students how they feel when they participate in this activity. You can also infuse fitness and wellness concepts during the brief rest quite readily.

5. Return to the freak-out.

SAFETY CONSIDERATIONS

Ensure the play area is free and clear of anything students can trip on or fall over. Students may become overheated, so leave a few moments at the end for an appropriate cool-down. The students should walk slowly around the room or move their bodies slowly in self-space. Usually a cool-down of two to three minutes is adequate.

TIPS AND VARIATIONS

You can add rules concerning what to do when the music stops. Have students stand in a circle, invite a few to the center, and have dance-offs where they can showcase their moves. You might also want to introduce circus squares or silks and have each student use them in a rhythmic way.

MONKEY BUSINESS

AIM

This game lets participants raid the "bananas" (beanbags) from the other teams' banana trees. This activity is primarily used to increase fitness, reinvigorate students, and promote wellness concepts. You may want to prepare health and wellness concept questions and write them on index cards before the activity.

ACTIVITY OBJECTIVES

1. Students will be able to move around the playing area while keeping both hands and feet on the floor and trying to steal bananas from the other team.

2. Students will be able to enjoy this activity for the sake of fun and fitness.

3. Students will be able to demonstrate respect and responsible behavior toward others while participating.

4. Students will be able to have the opportunity to engage in regular physical activity.

GRADE LEVELS   K-3

NHES STANDARDS   1, 2, 3, 4, 5, 7

NASPE STANDARDS   1, 2, 3, 4, 5, 6

SUGGESTED TIME REQUIREMENTS   10 minutes

MATERIALS NEEDED

Enough beanbags ("bananas") so that each group has about six; one pylon ("tree") and one hula hoop for each group

PROCEDURE

1. Separate students into groups of five or six.

2. Give each group a home tree denoted by a pylon and a hoop set on the floor. Spread the groups throughout the space.

3. Each group is given six bananas (beanbags), which are safely put into their tree.

4. When you say, "Go," all the monkeys must try to steal the tasty bananas (beanbags) from the other trees and return them to their own tree. Monkeys must move around the space keeping both hands and both feet on the floor at all times.

5. When they steal a banana, they can put it in their pockets and return to their own tree.

6. This can go on for a few minutes. Monkeys cannot guard their tree and must allow a competing monkey to steal from their tree.

7. The object is to see which group of monkeys can get the most bananas when time is out. You can use your judgment when to call time; this activity is exhausting.

SAFETY CONSIDERATIONS

Clear the play area so no one collides with chairs or desks. You may want to mark off the play perimeter with cones. Because students are moving around like monkeys, it is possible that fingers or hands can be stepped on; you may want them to remove their shoes. This activity is tiring, and some students may not have the fitness to participate too long; be aware of their limitations.

TIPS AND VARIATIONS

To make this more interesting, keep a few bananas on the side; monkeys can approach you during the play time and get bonus bananas—provided they answer a select question correctly. The questions can be simple: Why do we exercise? How many fruits are recommended daily? How many hours of sleep should you get? Any concept is acceptable as long as it is age appropriate and kept to a one-word answer. These bonus bananas cannot be stolen and should be distinguished by a different color. Once won, they are kept in the teams' trees. Students with disabilities can be in charge of the bonus questions (provide the answers on an index card) and bonus banana distribution.

BUILDERS AND BULLDOZERS

AIM

This activity is primarily used to increase fitness and reinvigorate the students. The secondary aim of this activity is for half of the class to work together as a team to build and the other half of the class to work together to knock down or bulldoze as many cones as they can in a set amount of time.

ACTIVITY OBJECTIVES

1. Students will demonstrate teamwork as they try to put up or knock down as many cones as possible.
2. Students will be able be able to identify that their individual efforts play a small but effective part in the team's success.
3. Students will be able to have the opportunity to engage in regular physical activity.

GRADE LEVELS   K-6

NHES STANDARDS   2, 4

NASPE STANDARDS   1, 2, 3, 4, 5, 6

SUGGESTED TIME REQUIREMENTS   5-10 minutes

MATERIALS NEEDED

Approximately one cone per participant (cones should be no less than 6 inches, or 15 cm, in height and as tall as you like)

PROCEDURE

1. Scatter the cones around the play area, standing some on their sides.

2. Divide the group into two teams; one group will be the builders and they are responsible for setting the cones upright.

3. The other half of the group are the bulldozers; they are responsible for knocking down the cones.

4. Both groups are trying to accomplish these goals simultaneously.

5. Students may not kick the cones over, nor are they allowed to defend or block any cones.

6. Hands must be used to put up (build) or knock down (bulldoze) cones.

7. This is a frenzied activity. Remind students not to run; rather, they can move quickly by walking fast.

8. Also remind them to keep their heads up so they can see where they are going. This is a timed event; most students get worked up quickly with this activity. Two minutes is usually enough for all ages.

9. After the allotted time, count the cones that are still standing and those that have been knocked over. The team with the most is the winner.

10. Have teams switch jobs to keep it interesting.

SAFETY CONSIDERATIONS
Students sometimes move around the space without looking up so collisions are likely; that is why there is no running in this activity. Remove any obstacles from the play area.

TIPS AND VARIATIONS
You might want to change the size of the cones (choose shorter ones) and the size of the play area (make it larger) to increase fitness levels. Smaller cones increase the effort needed; they are harder to set up and knock down because they are closer to the floor, particularly for the bigger children.

UNDER AND OVER RELAYS

AIM
This activity is primarily designed to increase health-enhancing levels of fitness, provide the opportunity for cooperative play, and allow participants to demonstrate responsible behaviors while having fun.

ACTIVITY OBJECTIVES
1. Students will be able to work as a team to accomplish predetermined tasks as quickly as they can.
2. Students will demonstrate their ability to use interpersonal communication skills to enhance the likelihood of success within this activity.
3. Students will be able to have the opportunity to engage in regular physical activity.

GRADE LEVELS   K-6

NHES STANDARDS   1, 4, 5, 6

NASPE STANDARDS   1, 2, 3, 4, 5, 6

SUGGESTED TIME REQUIREMENTS   5-10 minutes

MATERIALS NEEDED
An equal numbers of objects per group such as books, bowling pins, balled-up paper, beanbags, or balls; two hula hoops per group

PROCEDURE
1. Divide the students into groups of five or six. Have them stand in a line, one behind the other, with their legs apart and enough room between the students so that they can bend to the front and back without bumping into the person in front of or behind them.

2. All the objects to be passed are put in a pile at the start of the line; the hula hoops are placed at the end of the line. Once passed, objects must find their way to the hoop in order for a team to finish.

3. This is a simple relay; however, the objects must be passed under the legs of the first person to the hands of the second, who will then pass the object up and over his or her head to the third person in the line, who will then pass the object under his or her legs to the next in line, and so on.

4. Each team starts with the same number of articles to pass. The first team to pass all the articles to the end and place them in the hoop while following an under-and-over pattern wins.

SAFETY CONSIDERATIONS

Make sure students are far enough away from each other so they don't knock into each other. Make sure objects are not too heavy.

TIPS AND VARIATIONS

You might want to do this activity with a small heavy ball (one or two pounds) to increase fitness levels and challenge. Older students can pass heavier objects.

EXTREME HOT POTATO

AIM

This activity is primarily designed to increase health-enhancing levels of fitness, provide the opportunity for cooperative play and skill development, and allow participants to demonstrate responsible behaviors while having fun.

ACTIVITY OBJECTIVES

1. Students will play cooperatively while enhancing fitness.
2. Students will be able to engage in regular physical activity.
3. Students will be able to demonstrate respect and responsible behavior toward others while participating in this energizing activity.

GRADE LEVELS   K-6

NHES STANDARDS   4

NASPE STANDARDS   1, 2, 3, 4, 5, 6

SUGGESTED TIME REQUIREMENTS   5-10 minutes

MATERIALS NEEDED

Kindergarten through grade 2 can use beanbags and grades 3 to 6 can use weighted balls (use a medicine ball or put sand in a ball so that it weighs 2 to 4 pounds); two jump ropes

PROCEDURE

1. Hot potato involves players quickly gathering in a circle and tossing a beanbag or a weighted ball or small medicine ball to each other while music plays. The player who is holding the beanbag or ball (called the hot potato) when the music stops is out.

2. However, in Extreme Hot Potato this person has a choice of either stepping into the middle of the circle and skipping rope five times or stepping outside the circle and crab-walking the perimeter of the circle. After they are finished, they then return to their spot.

3. Play continues until everyone has had the hot potato.

4. If there are a lot of students, you can place two beanbags or weighted balls into play.

5. The game is designed to be fast-paced and high pressure. The game can also be played without music, and the group can sing traditional or original made-up rhymes.

SAFETY CONSIDERATIONS

Make sure the rope jumper stays in the center of the circle and does not throw the rope. Students who choose to crab-walk the perimeter should be far enough away from the circle so they don't get stepped on.

TIPS AND VARIATIONS

To add another element of fitness you can have students do a squat before passing the beanbag or ball to the next person. You can also have every other person facing outside the circle; when passing the beanbag or ball, the individual has to perform a trunk twist to receive the potato and one to give the potato away.

STOP, DROP, AND ROLL

AIM
This activity teaches fire safety behaviors while allowing students to be energized by the physical activity.

ACTIVITY OBJECTIVES
1. Students will be able to demonstrate how to react when they hear a smoke alarm.
2. Students will demonstrate how to react in the event of smoke being present.
3. Students will demonstrate the proper response in the event that they or their clothes catch fire.
4. Students will be able to participate in an activity that teaches life skills while enhancing their personal fitness.

GRADE LEVELS   K-3

NHES STANDARDS   1, 5, 7

NASPE STANDARDS   1, 2, 3, 4, 5, 6

SUGGESTED TIME REQUIREMENTS   15 minutes

MATERIALS NEEDED
Three or four yellow pinnies, two red pinnies, and two blue pinnies to denote the different jobs (you can also use colored bandannas, or you can create yellow, red, and blue badges that hang from the neck with yarn); four cones

PROCEDURE
1. This game is meant to be hurried so that participants must react quickly. Students should be told briefly about fire safety procedures—the stop, drop, and roll—and that their quick reaction in the case of fire is fundamental to their safety and health.

2. Place the four cones equidistant from each other around the play area; these represent the safety zone.

3. Choose three or four students to wear the yellow pinnies; they will be the firefighters.

4. Choose two players to be smoke and give them blue pinnies; choose two players to be fire and give them red pinnies.

5. All players start in a standing position in the middle of the play area.

6. Say, "Go," and all the participants move about the area, either walking or jogging.

7. The students with the red pinnies are fire; they tag the other participants and shout, "Fire!"

8. When this happens, the tagged player must stop, drop, and roll (one complete rotation) and stay still until a firefighter with a yellow pinny tags them.

9. Once students are tagged they can join the game again.

10. Students wearing blue pinnies are smoke; they shout, "Smoke!" when they tag a participant.

11. The participant must stop, crawl to safety (to one of the cones), and wait for a fireman to tag them free. They can then rejoin the activity.

12. After a few moments (three to four minutes is usually enough), you can have students switch positions and go again.

SAFETY CONSIDERATIONS
Because some students will be on the floor crawling and rolling, the others must pay careful attention not to step on or fall over someone.

TIPS AND VARIATIONS
You can vary this activity by changing the proportion of the participants wearing the different-colored pinnies. You can also eliminate one or two of the safety zone cones so that the students will have to work harder to get safe.